CONTENTS

Perspective on the Spirit

God gave me two pictures recently. One was of a child with cerebral palsy. We could look at that child and know that although the body was not entirely functional, the spirit was not diminished. The spirit was capable of being nurtured and becoming great, but it was trapped by the body, unable to express itself.

The second picture was of a person whose spirit was thin, tiny, undernourished, but the soul was the size of a sumo wrestler. The spirit had no chance to implement the will of God in this person's life because the soul had been so overfed for so long. The Scripture says, "Whoever has no rule over his own spirit is like a city broken down, without walls" (Proverbs 25:28 NKJV). A city that is broken down and without walls lacks clear identity, clear boundaries, and the means to protect itself. Similarly, someone who is controlled by his soul will not have the proper identity, nor will he have solid boundaries that will protect him. God designed our spirit to be dominant and the soul to be subordinate to the spirit, but when a culture feeds the soul and ignores the spirit, it develops a misrepresentation.

We must focus on speaking to our spirit and the spirit of others, asking God to bring into our lives a massive amount of challenge, nurture, stimulation, and direction for the spirit. A person's spirit should rule the soul, but it doesn't get there automatically or accidentally. The word "self-control" in the New Testament accurately portrays a spirit ruling over a soul. It is significant that this is the ninth fruit of the Spirit. A person must have all of the previous eight built into his spirit before that magnificent ninth fruit of the spirit can subdue the sumo wrestler-soul.

Arthur Burk

Introduction and Experience
by Sylvia Gunter

"May God himself, the God of peace, sanctify you through and through. May your whole spirit, soul and body be kept blameless at the coming of our Lord Jesus Christ. The one who calls you is faithful and he will do it" (1 Thessalonians 5:23-24).

For some time I have been praying based on 1 Thessalonians 5:23-24. I learned this from Arthur Burk based on his experience with praying for the spirit of babies in the womb. Since that time, he has enlarged the scope of his ministry to the spirit by praying for the spirits of adults. I first heard him do this on the Baby Blessings teaching, which is available on CD online at www.plumblineministries.com. I would put the joy blessings or peace blessings on and let them play continuously in my office or car. When I would come into the room at odd times or get into the car and pick up where it left off, I would hear just what I needed at that moment. What Arthur was praying right then was the boost my spirit needed. It was such a profound blessing to my spirit that I began praying these kinds of prayers for adults. Nobody I know received this blessing for their spirits at the crucial pre-birth time of development in their lives or even as children. I have seen God re-parent me and others using this kind of blessing and prayer. It is particularly profound in filling daddy holes.

Being filled with the Spirit means that God's Spirit in you infuses and controls your spirit, soul and body. When your spirit is controlled by His Spirit and is dominant over your soul, your whole person is conformed to God's truth and His intention for you. I have found that when your spirit is centered in joy and peace and is larger than your soul, it works to take care of a lot of other things, including lies you believe, depression, discouragement, death and destruction.

I know it works because it is God's idea. Do a Scripture study of the spirit of man and its roles and functions. How about these verses from Proverbs? "A man's spirit sustains him in sickness, but a crushed spirit who can bear?" (Proverbs 18:14) "A cheerful heart is good medicine, but a crushed spirit dries up the bones" (Proverbs 17:22). What about the spirit's role in worship? "...My soul glorifies the Lord and my spirit rejoices in God my Savior" (Luke 1:46-47). What about your spirit's role in understanding? "It is the spirit in a man, the breath of the Almighty, that gives him understanding" (Job 32:8). What about the spirit's role in hearing God's Spirit with the ears of our spirit? "He who has ears, let him hear" (Matthew 11:15). What about your spirit's role in will? "...The spirit is willing, but the body is weak" (Matthew 26:41). A full list of the Scriptures on the human spirit is at the end of this book.

> THE MOST PROFOUND BLESSING OUR SPIRIT NEEDS TO RECEIVE AND CAN RECEIVE IS THE FATHER-HEART OF GOD, HIS SPECIAL CREATION OF US, HIS KIND INTENTION TOWARD US, HIS MATCHLESS LOVE FOR US, HIS GLORY REVEALED IN US.

David in the Psalms records a conversation presumably between his soul and his spirit. He is clearly talking to himself in Psalms 42-43.

"These things I remember as I pour out my soul: how I used to go with the multitude, leading the procession to the house of God, with shouts of joy and thanksgiving among the festive throng. Why are you downcast, O my soul? Why so disturbed within me? Put your hope in God, for I will yet praise him, my Savior and my God. My soul is downcast within me..."

(Psalm 42:4-6).

JESUS WAS PREPARED, EMPOWERED, ANOINTED, AND APPOINTED BY GOD TO BRING GOOD NEWS TO OUR SPIRITS, TO RELEASE SLAVERY OF SPIRIT AND SOUL, TO GIVE US THE VISION OF BEING SONS...

The most profound blessing our spirit needs to receive and can receive is the Father-heart of God: His special creation of us, His kind intention toward us, His matchless love for us, His glory revealed in us. This is a gold mine of identity and legitimacy from which to live out our birthright confidently and purposefully. To know the Father-heart of God nurtures belonging, inclusion, and worth. This is exquisite fathering, and if it is received, will lead to exquisite sonship.

In the natural, a father calls a child to life. A father's role is to provide a safe, secure environment, but his deeper place is to call to life his child's real essence as a person. Our heavenly Father's heart is passionate for our full identity as sons. He calls our spirit to life to possess fully our due sonship. What is a son's nature? It is freedom, purity, nobility of character, confident identity, legal authority, purpose, access to the Father, deep intimacy with the Father and within His house, family likeness, and more.

Our Father is the judicial Ancient of Days, the ruling Lord and King, but He never stops being our Father to love, heal, comfort, deliver, and correct us for our good and His glory. He never loses His vision for whom He designed us to be. His Son Jesus began His ministry by defining His call and His eternal relationship with us. He said, "The Spirit of the Lord is on Me, because he has anointed me to preach good news to the poor. He has sent me to proclaim freedom for the prisoners and recovery of sight for the blind, to release the oppressed, to proclaim the year of the Lord's favor" (Luke 4:18-19).

The mission of Jesus was internal first, and His kingdom is now within us. Jesus was prepared, empowered, anointed, and appointed by God to bring good news to our spirits: to release slavery of spirit and soul; to give us the vision of being sons; to lift those who are downtrodden, bruised, crushed, and broken in spirit; and to call them forth to become the true sons that they are. For most of us, our soul dominates our spirit, because we have fed the soul a lifetime diet of lies through passivity of spirit and the constant bombardment of the world, the flesh, and the devil. We have exercised our soul far more than our spirit.

Our Father is working constantly to bring us to know fully our birthright as sons, and this is done by the Spirit of sonship, which indicates that sonship is a spirit-thing, first of all. Sonship is received in our spirit and works on our heart and soul to release us from sin and the flesh and to bring recovery from wounding. It also propels us forward into the potential that God wrote in His book for us, all the possibilities He planted in our DNA, both spiritually and naturally. The resurrection power of the Son is actively available to our spirit and working on our behalf. Our part is to cooperate with Him and not to quench Him. Jesus said that this is "...the day when salvation and the free favor of God profusely abound" (Luke 4:19, Amplified). He said that the Spirit

THE RESURRECTION POWER OF THE SON IS ACTIVELY AVAILABLE TO OUR SPIRITS AND WORKING ON OUR BEHALF.

of God is extending His favor toward us, assuring us release into a new status—the full rights of our true identity. Someone recently said that he had moved out of sin management mode into the presence of the grace of God. That is a spirit thing.

People whose spirit needs to be called to life and enlarged cannot meet God deeply, if at all. They cannot embrace life or themselves fully, and they cannot connect with the spirit and heart of another person. They feel isolated, going through the motions of life. Their conscience functions by remorse, regret, or fear of being caught or fear of punishment. Some of them have a reckless disregard for life. Some have to deaden their pain with addictions of all kinds, because their spirit cannot give them hope, comfort, and meaning. We all know the deadness of spirit that results in living by the law—by rote and rite, forms and legalism. 2 Timothy 3:5 describes it well, as "...having a form of godliness but denying its power...." These people mentally relate to doctrine and teaching and may receive soulish comfort and logical satisfaction in the liturgy or a "plan" of salvation, but there is no real spiritual spark. Religious flesh is soul-powered.

THE BLESSINGS OF THE FATHER ARE DESIGNED TO GET A PERSON'S SPIRIT IN TUNE WITH HIS/HER FATHER'S HEART OVER A 40-DAY PERIOD.

God our Father is rousing our spirit and waking the dead places in us, but it is not only our lives that are waking. We are being called to awaken the slumbering spirit in others. There will be a price to pay for waking the inert or shackled places in our spirit and bearing the burdens of calling to life the deadness in others. The crowd that gathered at the tomb of Lazarus was well aware of that, as Martha said, "He smells!" The stone had to be rolled away, and the gathered loved ones had to remove the grave clothes. Don't sanitize that picture. An unembalmed body had been in the hot sun of the Middle East for four days wrapped in linen strips. Yes, it was messy, stinky business. Yes, there will be pain for us as we minister to others what we have received, but it will be redemptive pain—birth pains.

These blessings are focused in two directions. The blessings of the Father are designed to get a person's spirit in tune with the Father's heart over a 40-day period. They are about identity, legitimacy, and birthright, and their by-products of joy, peace, patience, kindness, goodness, faithfulness, gentleness, and self-control. All these are necessary to living from the spirit of a life-giver in faith, hope, and love. The blessings focused on the names of God are intended to settle the spirit into the eternal realities of the magnificence, authority, and dominion of our God in whom we live, and move, and have our being.

> THE BLESSINGS FOCUSED ON THE NAMES OF GOD ARE INTENDED TO SETTLE THE SPIRIT INTO THE ETERNAL REALITIES OF THE MAGNIFICENCE, AUTHORITY, AND DOMINION OF OUR GOD...

I have two goals for those who are touched by these prayers.

1. I yearn for and pray for measurable growth in your spirit as a son—growth that translates mentally, spiritually, emotionally, and relationally. The Father's beloved Son "...grew in wisdom and stature, and in favor with God and men" (Luke 2:52). I want you to choose to disregard the slavemaster-accuser's lies about your adequacy, identity, legitimacy, etc. I envision measurable growth in spiritual discernment, spiritual character, fulfilling your birthright and potential, and relationships

with others—every area of covenantal life vertically and horizontally. Father God wants to do a deep and thorough work for those who are advancing in the likeness of His beloved Son.

2. I want you to consolidate and incarnate this truth for yourself, but I also want you to consolidate this truth for some people around you who do not know they are sons and are living like slaves. Where you are going is freedom: fulfillment, revelation of God's intention for you, and real life in the Spirit—everything that Jesus meant by the abundant life. The darkness or slumber where most people live provides the perfect backdrop for the rising glory of a perfectly awakened and enlarged spirit within. We are on the brink of something awesome in waking sleeping spirits. This is the time of the Father's favor, a time of release of the life of sonship, as we are closer to the days foretold in Malachi 4:5-6, "See, I will send you the prophet Elijah before that great and dreadful day of the LORD comes. He will turn the hearts of the fathers to their children, and the hearts of the children to their fathers; or else I will come and strike the land with a curse." Restoring horizontal relationships requires that the spirits of both parties be able to respond to each other because they are activated by the Spirit of the Lord.

In the South, we have an all-purpose phrase that is intended to be a genteel means of identification, affirmation, and comfort. "Bless your heart!" Be prepared to bless your spirit as Father God nurtures your spirit with blessings from His Word. I am praying that your Father God will awake, enlarge, and strengthen your spirit with these deposits of His blessings. I pray for many large-spirited people to come alongside you, for God will use the spirits of others to bless you as well. Look for them!

Testimonials & Feedback

I received these responses from people who used just one blessing, "Seeing the Fingerprints of God."

From a young lady who missed a retreat at which she was to speak because she had been ill for several weeks: *How perfect is the timing of our God! I feel so incredibly enlarged in spirit. I so see God's fingerprints in my life! I only wish you were here and you could read on my face what I cannot put in words yet. I am blessed.*

From a young man who is a seminary student and who also leads college students: *Man! That spoke to my spirit. That was incredible, and I read it over and over. I can't thank you enough.*

From a young lady suffering with deep depression as we prayed one of these over the phone: *I can see how this would affect people deeply.*

From one who has been walking with me through this praying/writing process: *I get it! I've been reading the blessings on a daily basis. Today I read all of them at the same time—POW! Something popped. Some I read out loud and some not. I get it! This enlarges my spirit. As my spirit is enlarged, it knows God as my Father more and more. It in turn takes my Father's truth and speaks to my soul. My soul in its wounded fathering and gaping holes of fathering receives healing from my spirit. I believe, not just know in my head, but believe. How awesome is that—I believe. I can't quit crying. Thank you. Let me repeat a thousand times thank you, and don't take out a single thank you. I get it!*

> I GET IT! THIS ENLARGES MY SPIRIT. AS MY SPIRIT IS ENLARGED, IT KNOWS GOD AS MY FATHER MORE AND MORE.

From another: *With each one my spirit rises with a new song from my Father. Thank you from all the children who do not know where to start. You have given us a safe place to be who Father intends us to be. I have always longed to hear those words spoken in just this manner. It reads like a love letter from my daddy. When I finish, I know I am valued, I have worth, and I am loved. Thank you.*

From another: *I wanted you to know that your blessings for my spirit have deeply impacted me. God has truly worked in these. I have been praying these for my daughter, and I have seen a definite change in her since I started to use them. I have seen the most amazing things happening with her in the last two weeks. I am starting afresh today to pray these for her every day. I asked the Lord to give me a friend to pray these prayers with, and we started this morning.*

From another: *If you want to be whole, your spirit has got to be free! Our mind is at enmity with God so we must develop a dynamic of victory and triumph within our spirit. Your prayers of blessing for my spirit are helping me do that. God is reviving my spirit. I'm still reading and absorbing and praying daily and can FEEL my spirit being set free!! When I call out my name(s) to speak to my spirit, I say my maiden name, name of first marriage and children's last name, and my present name and family. I have felt something happening the last few days when I do that but am not sure how to explain it. There were so many things that I was taught wrong when I was growing up as a girl, and God is going back to my childhood and my growing up days at home, and He is healing, reprogramming,*

GOD IS REVIVING MY SPIRIT. I'M STILL READING AND ABSORBING AND PRAYING DAILY AND CAN **FEEL** MY SPIRIT BEING SET FREE!!

and renewing my spirit! In my first marriage, both my children and I were abused and shamed, physically, verbally, mentally, emotionally and spiritually. I'm trusting God to heal all that in my spirit and to heal my children as well, since I am including them. I'm trusting Him to heal problems in my second marriage and with my second family.

The insights and wisdom and knowledge are phenomenal. I am amazed each day at things I'm learning about God through the daily blessings. They teach, train, and transform me as I pray them. They help me to "understand the times in order to know what to do," and they almost always just suit the very thing that my family and I need on that day. I feel so peaceful, content, and encouraged after reading just one blessing, and many times I read another one. I believe these are going to change the lives of people who read them in a dramatic way! These blessings will bring about immediate healing, transformation, and revelation.

From another: *I am getting so blessed from these blessings. Yesterday and the day before, I cried as I felt the Holy Spirit permeating into my spirit these truths and instructions in righteousness. God has been using me in my city to organize and lead city-wide prayer on a weekly basis. I have intercessors, city employees, city councilmen, pastors, firemen, police, business people, and people in ministry getting involved. The blessing of having a leader to implement the necessary components to do the job, having all the people necessary to help bring revival into my city and family—wow! I can't tell you how much this is helping me.*

Today I cried again as I was blessed about peacemaking skills and shoes of peace. I've always been a peacemaker and am so delighted to receive a blessing for improving my skills to hear my Father and improving the art of peacemaking. My husband is constantly stirring up division, alienation, chaos. The Lord showed me that he was trained to be a man of war, and he still seems to be of that mindset. He's making war one minute, and the next minute acting as if it never happened and being very peaceful. It seems that he gets confused and thinks I'm the enemy and he must defend himself against me. My way of protecting myself has been to isolate myself, but the Lord is helping me to forgive more quickly from my spirit and forget the abrasive words. I've started declaring that I am not going backward; I am moving forward. I have the victory in my spirit, and I am not going to let it rob me of my peace and joy. One statement that brought so much healing is, 'I bless you with endurance in peace-making because being a peacemaker is a difficult thing.' I say AMEN to that.

I CRIED AS I FELT THE HOLY SPIRIT PERMEATING INTO MY SPIRIT THESE TRUTHS AND INSTRUCTIONS IN RIGHTEOUSNESS.

This one is so special I have to include it in its entirety. One day, I was reading the account of Jesus' baptism in Mark. I noticed the Father's words are different in Mark than in Matthew. Matthew 3:17 says, "This is my Son, whom I love; with whom I am well pleased." This was the wording I was most familiar with: "This is my Son" (third person). I thought the Father was sort of introducing Jesus to the world—like "TA DA! (Drum roll, please.) Take note, all inhabitants of earth. Your life is about to get mighty interesting. I'm about to do something BIG for you!" But Mark 1:11 says, "You are my Son, whom I love; with you I am well pleased." The Father spoke directly to Jesus, second person. It was personal, not a general announcement.

I began wondering why the Father addressed Jesus so personally. It made sense for Father God to say these things about Jesus to bystanders. But why say them to Jesus? On the face of it, none of this was new information to Jesus. Scripture reveals that Jesus knew He was God's Son while at the temple as a 12-year-old.

As Jesus was the visible image of His invisible Father and someone with an impeccable command of the Old Testament, I would assume no one needed to tell Him that He was the offspring of a loving Father. And, of course, the Father was well-pleased with Him. Any father should be extremely pleased with a sinless, perfect son.

I was mystified. Why did the Father say these things to Jesus?

Later, as I was praying, I heard myself say something like, "Thank you for telling Jesus how you felt about Him, for feeding Him with your words." I went on to say I longed to hear words like that myself and wish I had heard them from one of my parents. How fortunate Jesus was to have heard them! Something silently rumbled inside. This was the wound. Most of the words I heard from my toxic parents were the opposite of these words—the spoken ones and the unspoken ones.

As I continued to pray, I realized the Father was nourishing Jesus. He was feeding Him vital emotional nutrients. And doing it so the whole world could take note! If Jesus needed this nourishment from His Father, how much more do we! Our sin, and the sin of others, drains us of essential nutrients.

Then I noticed Mark 1:12-13, "At once the Spirit sent him out into the desert, and he was in the desert 40 days, being tempted by Satan." His Father fed Jesus before He fasted and confronted the devil. In Matthew 4:4, Jesus says in response to the first *temptation, "It is written: 'Man does not live on bread alone, but on every word that comes from the mouth of God.'" I previously thought He was referring to Scripture as "every word that comes from the mouth of God," but I now think He was talking about the actual words of nourishment the Father spoke into His being. I was blown away at this picture of the Father feeding His Son before a potentially draining experience!*

Day 1 Identity and Legitimacy

   [Fill in the name], I call your spirit to attention in the name of Jesus of Nazareth. Listen with your spirit to God's Word for you. "For you created my inmost being; you knit me together in my mother's womb. I praise you because I am fearfully and wonderfully made; your works are wonderful, I know that full well. My frame was not hidden from you when I was made in the secret place. When I was woven together in the depths of the earth, your eyes saw my unformed body. All the days ordained for me were written in your book before one of them came to be" (Psalm 139:13-16).

   _____, your Father made you special. You are a very special person, created and crafted and designed by God your Father. Before the foundation of the world, your Father planned for you. You are no accident. You did not have to exist, but your Father willed you into existence. He chose the day and the time you would start your life. He chose your parents and wove you together in your mother's womb. He planned your birth order and put you in your family. He chose every one of your 23 pairs of chromosomes. He chose every one of your 10,000 plus genes. He chose every part of your spiritual heritage. He reached back into your father's bloodline and your mother's bloodline, and from generations past, your heavenly Father chose different parts of your heritage. Some parts are not so beautiful, and some parts are absolutely gorgeous. Yet your Father wove it all together and gave you everything you need in the package of your life to be an overcomer,

1

a victor, to take the negative parts of your heritage and triumph over them, to walk in the beauty of all that God has placed within you.

Your Father made you beautiful and beloved. I bless you, _____, because you are fearfully and wonderfully made. God invested an incredible amount of effort and concentration in designing you. You are unique, one of a kind. There is nobody else like you. God has thought extensively about you. Every detail of your body, every organ, and every cell is the result of God's thoughts. Every facet of your personality is the result of His kind intention. You are beautiful, and you are beloved. God has blessed you with His love. God smiled on the day He created you. He had been waiting for millennia for the particular point in time when you were conceived. He had great joy in His heart when His plans actually came together. He nurtures your spirit; He watches over you.

THERE IS A SPIRITUAL TREASURE CHEST OF GENERATIONAL BLESSINGS WITH YOUR NAME ON IT.

Your world needs you. You bring something to your family that no other person has. They need the gifts you bring. Your family would not be complete without you. Others in your circle need the deposit that God has placed in your life.

_____, your Father wrote your days in His book. He has already read the final chapters, although we have not had that privilege. Your life is not a random thing. He is looking forward to the chapters of the story He has already written. He designed your spiritual heritage. Your generational blessings go back a thousand generations. There is a spiritual treasure chest of generational blessings with your name on it. Those are being released to you incrementally over the course of your life at the appointed, appropriate time. All this is God's master plan. God has foreseen your pain. He promises that because of His love, His power, and His blessing upon you, He causes pain and negative things to be transformed into good things before the end of the story of your life. We don't know everything about who you are going to be or what you are going to do, but you are loved, you are a blessing to your family, and you are a life-giver in the world. You are special, and we celebrate God's miraculous design of who you are. I bless you in the name of Jesus of Nazareth.

Respond with your spirit...

Write your thoughts, etc.

Day 2 Knowing Your Purpose

_____, I call your spirit to attention in the name of Jesus of Nazareth. Listen with your spirit to God's promise in His Word. "For we are God's workmanship, created in Christ Jesus to do good works, which God prepared in advance for us to do" (Ephesians 2:10). Your Father has a purpose for you. I bless you with knowing your purpose as God has seen it in His heart. I bless you with being everything that God has designed you to be, because as you experience the joy of fulfilling your purpose, you will benefit, others will benefit, and the world will be blessed.

_____, I bless you with fulfilling the call of God on your life and living out the fullness of His will. I bless you with being in your Father's time, not running ahead and not lagging behind, but knowing His will and doing His will in the right time, the right place, and the right way, with the right people alongside you. I bless you with knowing the things your Father has called you to know and doing the things that He has called you to do. I bless you with being able to carry out God's work with honor, with peace, with joy, doing God's work, God's way. He has uniquely designed you as an instrument of a particular set of good deeds. You can do them better than anybody else can do them because your Father has uniquely positioned you. I come into agreement with God and with His Word, and I bless His design of you. I bless the good works that have your name on them for you to do, and I bless the way your Father has

> I BLESS YOU WITH BEING EVERYTHING THAT GOD HAS DESIGNED YOU TO BE, BECAUSE AS YOU EXPERIENCE THE FULFILLING JOY OF BEING WHO GOD HAS DESIGNED YOU TO BE, AS YOU FULFILL YOUR PURPOSE, YOU WILL BENEFIT, OTHERS WILL BENEFIT, AND THE WORLD WILL BE BLESSED.

designed you to do them. I invest in you, I care for you, I love you, I nurture you, for you are a treasure and a blessing to the world.

I bless you with a life-giving community to fit into. You have a piece to put into a mosaic, and I bless you with fitting together with other people, because you can't do what God has called you to do alone. I bless you with finding like-hearted, like-visioned, like-spirited others. I bless you with being a part of a family of ministry where you can enjoy your greatest fulfillment as you fit with other people who are finding their fulfillment in God's purposes, and each of you is doing what God has designed you to do.

> YOUR FATHER INTENDS FOR YOU TO HAVE BEAUTY OF SPIRIT. I BLESS YOU WITH FULFILLMENT, GRACE, ELEGANCE, THE WISDOM AND BEAUTY OF HEAVEN.

Your Father will bless you, _____, with the right closed doors, because your enemy will try to get you to do things that God has not designed you to do—good things, legitimate things, profitable things, honorable things, but your Father has not designed you to do them. I bless you with not wasting time or effort in doing things that God has not called you to do, but being able to invest fully where God is positioning you and being fully present to today's grace and today's assignment. Your Father will bless you with open doors to walk forward in His time, in His calling, for you to experience the joy of fulfillment of being everything He has called you to be at the right time and in the right place.

Your Father intends for you to have beauty of spirit. I bless you with fulfillment, grace, elegance, and the wisdom and beauty of heaven. I celebrate the beauty that God has nurtured in you. You are God's craftsmanship, His masterpiece, His poem. You are not just a piece of a puzzle, a tool designed to function, to do good works just because the world needs them done and the kingdom of God will be advanced. I bless you with obeying Him one day at a time with beauty of spirit, an ease of effort, and the favor of His making a way.

Your Father intends for you to carry the fragrance of heaven, for people to be attracted to you. It will not happen because you are effective, or competent, or secure, or have a holy boldness about you, but because you have the perfume of heaven. I bless you, _____, with being a fragrant offering as you do the work God wants you to do. I bless you in the name of Jesus of Nazareth.

Respond with your spirit...
Write your thoughts, etc.

Day 3 Knowing Life-Givers

_____, I call your spirit to attention in the name of Jesus of Nazareth. Listen to the Word of the Lord for you. "But why am I so favored, that the mother of my Lord should come to me? As soon as the sound of your greeting reached my ears, the baby in my womb leaped for joy. Blessed is she who has believed that what the Lord has said to her will be accomplished!" (Luke 1:43-45)

When two people meet, there is an exchange of energy. There are life-givers who release energy into your soul, and others who receive energy from you. There was so much of the life of God and the Spirit of God around Mary that when she came into the presence of Elizabeth and of John the Baptist in her womb, their spirits leapt for joy.

_____, you are an emotional life-giver, but it is so much better to be a spiritual life-giver. Your Father designed you to receive life-giving and to be spiritually life-giving. Your Father will bring you people who will cause your spirit to leap for joy. I bless you with not always being in the presence of people who are draining your spirit, but may God frequently bless you with people who minister to your spirit, people who have so much anointing around them, that your spirit responds. I bless you with divine appointments where God connects you for a moment or an hour with mighty men and women of God. In those times you will experience joy, enlargement, enrichment, and anointing of your spirit as you are in the presence of faith-filled, Spirit-filled people. I bless you with God's bringing to you men and women who are pure, who lift up holy hands, whose lives are not only disciplined but dominated by the presence of God.

_____, your Father intends for you to experience godly dominion. I bless you with being blessed in your spirit by the spirit of people who walk in dominion, regardless of whether they are recognized by the world as having organizational or institutional authority. They know who they are; they know their identity. They have a strong sense of legitimacy, so they walk in godly authority: subduing the demonic and bringing in the presence of God; lifting up those things which are bowed down; healing the broken; creating a broad place for the glory of God to flow. I bless you with being with people like that who can teach you and model for you what dominion is. May your spirit leap for joy and celebrate the blessing that comes from walking shoulder to shoulder with mighty men and women of God who serve our King and who have been blessed by the King with His overcoming authority.

I BLESS YOU WITH BEING CONTAGIOUS WITH THE JOY OF THE LORD. I BLESS YOU WITH HAVING SO MUCH OF HIS JOY THAT YOUR JOY TOUCHES EVERYBODY YOU ASSOCIATE WITH...

Your Father intends for you to walk with those who know God's favor. I bless you with living alongside those who know the favor of God, who have experienced God's opening doors before them day in and day out. They understand God's moving obstacles out of the way, and God's preparing each moment of each day for them, to walk with settled peace in their spirits, because they know who they are and they know that the favor of God rests upon them. I bless you with drawing life-giving strength from their spirits as you experience the joy of associating with people who know the joy of a clear path before them. I bless you with God's frequently bringing to you those people who walk in the favor of God.

Your Father intends for you to be contagious with His joy. I bless you with being contagious with the joy of the Lord. I bless you with having so much of His joy that your joy touches everyone with whom you associate, and you leave behind you a trail of joy everywhere you go.

I bless you with significantly introducing people to the genuine joy of life with God. I bless you to transfer the joy of the presence of God, as others walk with you and draw from the abundance of the joy of the Lord in your spirit, and they are able to savor that themselves. I bless you with companionship with those who know the joy of the Lord, with God bringing joyful people to you to strengthen your spirit with joy. May your joy stir them up; may their joy stir you up, that you may be mutually life-giving. I bless you in the name of Jesus of Nazareth.

Respond with your spirit...

Write your thoughts, etc.

Day 4 God Fights for You

_____, I call your spirit to attention in the name of Jesus of Nazareth. Listen to the Word of God for you. "...Do not be afraid. Stand firm and you will see the deliverance the Lord will bring you today. The Egyptians you see today you will never see again. The Lord will fight for you; you need only to be still'" (Exodus 14:13-14).

_____, your Father intends for you to rest at peace in Him as He takes care of your enemies. I bless you with an unafraid heart that will lead you to the place of peace where God will fight for you and you will not have to fight. You will watch God remove your enemies before your eyes and deliver you. You will stand or move forward doing the things God has called you to do, and He will fight your battles. I bless you with daily steps of obedience, both in little things and in radical, unthinkable things that will position you for God to fight your battles for you.

Before He destroyed their enemies, your Father wanted His people to have great peace. I bless you with a large perspective of the peace that God wants for you.

I BLESS YOU WITH SEEING THE PRESENCE OF GOD IN THOSE THINGS THAT THE WORLD CALLS PROBLEMS AND PAIN.

I bless you with circumstances that are orchestrated by God to bring about the elimination of your enemies. I bless you with situations that only God could contrive: where you do nothing; where you don't need to battle; where you stand and watch and see God bring a problem right up to you and resolve the problem, so that your enemies are no longer there and will not return. I bless you with your Father's orchestrated situations and faith to see His provisions and not fear when problems come close to you.

Listen again with your spirit to the Word of the Lord for you. "Without faith it is impossible to please God, because anyone who comes to him must believe that he exists and that he rewards those who earnestly seek him" (Hebrews 11:6). Your Father intends for you to please Him with great faith. I bless you with the joy of imparting to other people the faith to walk in security in Him. I bless you with stories of God's intervention that are so deeply woven into your spirit that your sharing those stories with others lifts them up and out of fear and enables them to have the faith to look forward, to cry out for God's intervention in their own lives.

I bless you with being led by the Spirit to respond to problems with faith, not as a slave out of a victim mindset of avoidance, blame-shifting, or rationalization. I bless you with perseverance, not a spirit of fainting and giving up. I bless you with embracing problems, viewing them as challenges, and as opportunities for faith, as new ways to see the many facets of God and how He will work in them and through them to work things out in His plan.

I bless you with seeing the presence of God in those things that the world calls problematic and painful. I bless you with such faith that you can rejoice in standing firm as danger gets closer and you see God intervene on your behalf in a supernatural way, setting you free and removing your enemies so they will not again intrude on your life. I bless you with having the faith to look beyond the immediate price and see the treasure that lies on the other side. I bless you with receiving the reward of those who earnestly seek him.

_____, listen again with your spirit to the Word of God. "When a man's ways are pleasing to the Lord, he makes even his enemies live at peace with him" (Proverbs 16:7). Your Father intends for even your enemies to see that your ways are pleasing to Him. This is the highest level of God's protection, where your enemies want to be at peace with you. I bless you with that degree of the favor of the Lord upon your life, so that it will be evident that you have an intimate relationship with God and that God is with you. I bless you with people recognizing the favor of God upon your life without being jealous of His blessings on you. I pray that as they recognize His favor, the fear of the Lord will come upon them, and there will be a holy awe that a person could walk with God on such a level of intimacy.

I bless you with having the favor of God upon you in such a way that people will recognize that there is something different about your spirit, and they will come to you and seek to be at peace with you, because they do not want to offend the God with whom you are in a relationship. I bless you with having people verify and validate the favor of God upon you.

I bless you with your ways being pleasing to the Lord in such a profound way that your enemies live at peace with you and seek out your God. I bless you with having peace upon you that is a beacon in a world that is full of turmoil. I bless you with attracting people to you who are seeking safety and a relationship with the God with whom you have a relationship. They will seek to know your God who gives you such favor.

I bless you, _____, with the ultimate protection of peace, which is what God offers to those who walk with Him in His favor. I bless you with having your enemies be at peace with you, because they recognize God's hand. I bless you with these blessings in the name of Jesus of Nazareth.

Respond with your spirit...

Write your thoughts, etc.

Day 5 Sonship

_____, I call your spirit to attention. Listen with your spirit to the Word of God for you. "Those who are led by the Spirit of God are sons of God. For you did not receive a spirit that makes you a slave again to fear, but you received the Spirit of sonship. And by him we cry, 'Abba, Father.' The Spirit himself testifies with our spirit that we are God's children. Now if we are children, then we are heirs—heirs of God and co-heirs with Christ, if indeed we share in his sufferings in order that we may also share in his glory. I consider that our present sufferings are not worth comparing with the glory that will be revealed in us" (Romans 8:14-18).

_____, the Spirit of your Father gives witness that you are His son and are led by His Spirit. I bless you, _____, with the Spirit of sonship and the mindset of sonship. I bless you with embracing problems with the confidence that God is in them to give you grace to solve them and to overcome. I bless you with deep heart identity as God's very own child, securely loved in his family, calling him "Abba, dear Father." I bless you with the Spirit of sonship that does not make you a slave to fear because you know your Abba is with you. I bless you with the settled assurance that He has a future and a hope for you, that He has written your days in His book with love, for your best interests and His ultimate glory. I bless you with being filled with the deep knowledge that your Abba knows what you need and has all the resources of the universe to meet that need.

> I BLESS YOU WITH DEEP HEART IDENTITY AS GOD'S VERY OWN CHILD, SECURELY LOVED IN HIS FAMILY, CALLING HIM "ABBA, DEAR FATHER."

Listen again, _____, with your spirit to the Word of God for you. "The Spirit himself testifies with our spirit that we are God's children." I bless you with ears to hear the testimony of the Spirit of the Lord—the Spirit of wisdom and understanding, the Spirit of counsel and power, the Spirit of knowledge and the fear of the Lord. I bless you with delighting in obedience in the fear of the Lord. I bless you with the Spirit of God at home in you so that you will not judge by what you see with your eyes, mere appearance, or false evidence, or decide by what you hear with your ears or by deceptive conclusions. I bless you with being tuned into God with eyes for seeing and ears for listening according to His Spirit. I bless you with being led by the fullness of the Spirit of truth to call forth God's true spiritual discernment to see things as He sees them in the spirit realm.

I BLESS YOU WITH DEEP KNOWLEDGE THAT YOU ARE AN HEIR WITH YOUR BROTHER JESUS TO ALL THE TREASURIES OF YOUR FATHER.

Listen again with your spirit to the Word of God for you. "Now if we are children, then we are heirs—heirs of God and co-heirs with Christ, if indeed we share in his sufferings in order that we may also share in his glory." I bless you with deep knowledge that you are an heir with your brother Jesus to all the treasuries of your Father. I bless you with confidence that you have the riches of your Father and that you lack nothing that you need emotionally, physically, practically, mentally, spiritually, in any way. I bless you with embracing the fellowship of the sufferings of Jesus, so that you will be blessed with sharing His glory. I bless you with realizing the glory that you have and embracing the glory that you are.

Listen again, _____, with your spirit to the Word of God for you. "I consider that our present sufferings are not worth comparing with the glory that will be revealed in us." I bless you with the sure understanding that His ways are not our ways, and He wants to have His way for your good and His glory. I bless you with pressing forward to see the glory that He is revealing. I bless you as you listen every day as the Lord gives you the tongue of one being taught, "an instructed tongue, to know the word that sustains the weary" (Isaiah 50:4). I bless you with the beauty, satisfaction, and fulfillment of your Father wakening your ears morning by morning, opening your ears to be taught by Him, and I bless you with presenting to Him a heart that does not rebel or shrink away from what He puts before you day by day. I bless you with hunger for His glory every day, as you search Him out in His Word and watch and listen every day at the doorpost of the counsels of His wisdom. I bless you with glimpses of His glory revealed to you. I bless you in the name of Jesus of Nazareth.

Respond with your spirit...

Write your thoughts, etc.

Day 6 God's Presence

_____, I call your spirit to attention in the name of Jesus of Nazareth. I bless you with the joy of the Lord. Listen to God's Word for you. "You have made known to me the path of life; you will fill me with joy in your presence, with eternal pleasures at your right hand" (Psalm 16:11).

_____, you have experienced many different kinds of joy—joy of parental love, of friends and relationships, of accomplishment, of seeing God work in and through you, of seeing other people empowered to accomplish things. Your Father designed you to experience a vast number of joys that are legitimate, good, and wonderful. I bless you, _____, with your life being full of many different kinds of joy. I bless you with the greatest joy that comes from experiencing the presence of God in your spirit. I bless your spirit as a sanctuary, not a war zone, a safe place, a place where you are visited by the Holy Spirit, where He broods over your spirit and you become intensely familiar with the presence of God with you. I bless you with sensing His presence watching over your life. I bless you with experiencing the joy of His presence in both private and public worship.

Psalm 16:7 says, "...even at night, my heart instructs me." I bless you, _____, with fullness of joy in the night watches as the Spirit of God ministers to your spirit. The nighttime is the first-fruits of God's creation; therefore it is holy. I reject and break off of you every claim of the enemy to the night hours. I proclaim that it is God's holy time when He delights to visit you and to minister to you. I bless you with experiencing His presence in the night watches as your subconscious mind and your spirit are open to the Spirit of God, so He can minister to your spirit while your conscious mind is not cluttering up the works.

I bless you as your Father makes known the path of life to you. I bless you with joy as you see His presence in the world around you, His fingerprints on your own life, what He has prepared for you, the gifts that He has given you, the surprises that He has planned for you, the unexpected treasures He has placed in your life. In the name of Jesus of Nazareth, I anoint your eyes with ointment from Revelation 3:18 to see in the Spirit realm things as they are—the gifts and the presence and hand of God, His truth, and His love touches all through your life, day after day.

I bless you, _____, with going to different places around the world where God is working. In every generation there are unique visitations of the Spirit of God in different parts of the world. Each visitation has its particular expression of the presence and power of God. I bless you with having the liberty to travel, the ability to go and experience new and different flavors of the manifest presence of God. I bless you with being there and soaking in it, savoring it.

I bless you with the eternal pleasures at the right hand of your Father, the hand of authority and blessings. I bless you with hearing Him call you the beloved child of His right hand, His favorite child. I bless you with knowing that you bring Him pleasure. I bless you with a profound sense of the pleasure of your Father, as your heart is deeply pleased in Him. I bless you with the fullness of joy of the presence of the true and living God, in the name of Jesus of Nazareth.

Respond with your spirit...

Write your thoughts, etc.

Day 7 Trust

_____, I call your spirit to attention in the name of Jesus of Nazareth. Listen to God's Word for your spirit. "You will keep in perfect peace him whose mind is steadfast, because he trusts in you. Trust in the Lord forever, for the Lord, the Lord, is the Rock eternal" (Isaiah 26:3-4).

The word "trust" is very significant in the Old Testament. It is not an act of your will, where you choose to risk something, but it is a profound emotional confidence, in which you are completely expecting things to be right. It is like the trust that you felt in the womb as you listened to your mother's heart beat. You heard the thumping on a regular basis, your body vibrated with a rushing sound of blood as her heart pumped. You trusted in your mother's heart, for it continued to beat minute after minute, day after day, and you had complete emotional confidence in it. That is what the your Father wants you to experience with Him. He wants you to experience so much of His faithfulness that you are emotionally at peace in Him. There is a time and a place for risking on God as an act of faith, even when your emotions don't agree, but it is far greater, a more wonderful special gift, for you to trust and be truly at peace with what your Father is going to do and what He has called you to do.

So, _____, since this is God's will, and since this is your birthright, I bless you with having perfect peace that comes from trusting in the Lord. I bless you with experiencing your Father's faithfulness, His faithful love toward you, even when others do not love you or do not consider you lovely. I bless you with experiencing His love, for your emotions to be aware, to know, to savor, to feel, to relish the love that your Father expresses toward you. I bless you with experiencing that so often that you can never doubt your Father's love.

I bless you with experiencing your Father's faithfulness in providing for you. Your needs change, and your provision will come from many different sources. I bless you with seeing your Father provide again and again, so that you can have complete emotional confidence that He will provide your daily bread.

I bless you with having perfect peace about your Father's communication with you. He will speak at times through his Word very clearly and personally to you. At times He will be silent, and even His Word will seem closed and dry, but I bless you with perfect confidence and perfect peace during the silences of God, as you stand on the things He has said to you in the past. I bless you with no anxiety in the present because God has spoken so richly in the past. I bless you with the surety of knowing that He will speak again at the right time and the right place, that you will hear clearly what you need to hear at the right time to make the right decisions.

> I BLESS YOU WITH NO ANXIETY IN THE PRESENT BECAUSE GOD HAS SPOKEN SO RICHLY IN THE PAST.

I bless you, _____, with feeling perfect peace over the timing of God in all things. I bless you with experiencing your Father's supernatural timing over and over, for you to savor, deep in your spirit, His faithfulness in being, providing, arriving, communicating, and changing things at exactly the right time. I bless you with having your mind steadfast on the memories of God's past faithfulness, so that when you come up against what appears to be a crisis situation where He has not moved yet, you will have perfect peace that He will move at exactly the right time because you have experienced His timely faithfulness in the past.

I bless you, _____, with seeing where your Father has protected you. I bless you with perfect peace because you trust in your Father's protection of you. I bless you with experiencing His protection in the danger that comes near but does not touch you. I bless you with firsthand knowledge of your Father's infinite creativity in rescuing you from harm. I bless you with having your eyes opened to see circumstances and situations where the enemy set a trap that you didn't see, and your Father in His infinite wisdom and power removed the trap before you were aware of it. I bless you with growing experiences of His protecting your spirit, your soul, your body, and the call upon your life. I bless you with seeing so much of His protection that you will trust Him as implicitly as you trusted your mother's heartbeat. I bless you, _____, with having a mind that is set on Christ, who offers this peace. I bless you in the name of Jesus of Nazareth.

Respond with your spirit...

Write your thoughts, etc.

Day 8 Joy of the Lord

_____, I speak to your spirit in the name of Jesus of Nazareth. Listen with your spirit to the Word of God for you. "...Go and enjoy choice food and sweet drinks, and send some to those who have nothing prepared. This day is sacred to our Lord. Do not grieve, for the joy of the Lord is your strength" (Nehemiah 8:10).

During the reconstruction of the broken walls of Jerusalem, Nehemiah wanted the people to experience the joy that the Father was experiencing, because when they could tap into the joy that God experienced over what they had done so far, they would have the strength to walk the next mile and press on. There was a great deal of work yet to be done on the broken-down city. Much social woundedness needed to be healed, and there was much from God's Word that they had not experienced.

_____, I bless you with knowing the joy of the LORD that is your strength. I bless you with knowing joy in His Fatherness in profound and life-giving ways. I bless you with remembering times when He showed you His Fatherness. I bless you with enlarging your spirit to know profoundly and deeply that your Father is pleased with you. I bless you with receiving the truth of your identity, legitimacy, and birthright. I bless you with knowing who you are in your Father's eyes and with drinking deeply of the joy that He has in who you are.

I bless you with absorbing with your spirit the great detail of God your Father in sending an angel to one young woman to tell her that she had found favor with Him and would give birth to Jesus Christ the Messiah. Before that moment, she had no idea of her favor in the Father's eyes, how much He enjoyed her and how pleased He was with her. The joy that the Lord had in her gave her the strength to walk through the difficult months ahead. I bless you with knowing that kind of joy for difficult times and circumstances.

I bless you, _____, with receiving truth from the life of Gideon, who did not know that God looked upon him with favor. Gideon saw himself so poorly that he was hiding. He had no idea that God knew he existed, but God saw him as the mighty warrior He had designed before the foundation of the world to deliver Israel from the hand of the Midianites. I bless you with joy in a touch from God to seal in your heart and your spirit that you have favor in His eyes, AND that He will communicate His purposes for you that cannot be defeated.

I bless you with experiencing the joy that your Father has when your spirit rises up and responds to the Holy Spirit. I bless you with knowing the joy that your Father has when He sees that today you are different than you were yesterday. I bless you with feeling the joy that your Father has as He thinks out into the future of all the blessings that He has prepared—the surprises, the divine encounters, the unexpected treasures that He has prepared for you. I bless you with experiencing the joy of your Father in His anticipation over the road you are going to walk.

I bless you, _____, with savoring your Father's excitement over your design, each thing He has placed in you to do, your giftings. As those divine encounters are positioned, as you step up to possess your birthright to be a life-giver, I bless you with experiencing the joy He feels in knowing that the unique person that He has designed is cooperating with Him in the works that He has planned for you to do.

I bless you with fulfilling the joy of God who is leading you to do right things at the right time in the right way with the right people. I bless you with knowing and being so tuned to the Spirit of God that you know intuitively in your spirit what the right place is, what you are supposed to be doing, and how you are supposed to do it.

I bless you, _____, with knowing the joy of the Lord that gives you the strength to press on, go forward, to endure hardship as a good soldier, to accomplish, to fulfill, to prepare thoroughly, and to face pain unflinchingly. I bless you with knowing so profoundly the pleasure that He has in you that the opposition of other people means nothing, that you rebound from disappointment and return quickly to your joy center in your Father. I bless you with overcoming the pain, sorrow, shame, discouragement, and every sort of negative emotion in having to make a course correction, and I bless you to savor the joy that the Father has in you as you come back to the high joy level He designed for you.

_____, your Father made you. He master-planned you, uniquely designed for this particular time in history. He chose the time in history, the family that He placed you into, and all your days up to now. His craftsmanship of you and His plans for you will stand before His throne for all eternity. I bless you with having abiding strength to be where God has placed you and to accomplish what He has called you to do, because you are able to drink deeply of the joy that God the Father has in you, as His beloved handiwork, crafted for His pleasure and purposes. I bless you in the name of Jesus of Nazareth.

Respond with your spirit...
Write your thoughts, etc.

Day 9 Kingdom Of Peace

_____, I speak to your spirit in the name of Jesus of Nazareth. Listen to the Word of God for you. "The people walking in darkness have seen a great light; on those living in the land of the shadow of death a light has dawned. You have enlarged the nation and increased their joy; they rejoice before you as people rejoice at the harvest, as men rejoice when dividing the plunder. For to us a child is born, to us a son is given, and the government will be on his shoulders. And he will be called Wonderful Counselor, Mighty God, Everlasting Father, Prince of Peace. Of the increase of his government and peace there will be no end. He will reign on David's throne and over his kingdom, establishing and upholding it with justice and righteousness from that time on and forever. The zeal of the Lord Almighty will accomplish this" (Isaiah 9:2-3, 6-7). "I form the light and create darkness, I bring prosperity and create disaster; I, the Lord, do all these things" (Isaiah 45:7).

_____, you are under the protection of God who can do the impossible. I bless you with peace that comes from God who created light in great darkness, who brings light into the very shadow of death. I bless you with knowing that God makes peace regardless of your circumstances. You are living in troublesome days, when governments of the world are turning frequently to war, when terrorism is increasing and there is much uncertainty. The earth is convulsed; there are judgments from God, and iniquity is increasing. Many circumstances that you will face in your life are not conducive to peace. Although you are living in a sober time in history, you can walk in the light because God decrees that the light of His presence shines in darkness.

I bless you, _____, with not being dependent on circumstances in your world, but receiving from your Father the peace that He offers in your life, no matter how dark it is around you. I bless you with peace that can only come because the Prince of Peace rules you. I bless you with understanding the kingship of the Prince of Peace and the willingness to bow your knee and submit to Him. I bless you with seeing the kingdom of peace established in your life, for the Prince of Peace is your ruler. Everything you touch is part of His dominion, and His exercise of the rule of peace in your life grows larger from day to day. I bless you with peace that He decrees in your life and around your life. I bless you with experiencing the difference between living in the kingdom of light and peace and living in the kingdom of darkness.

I bless you with an anointing for taking the peace of the Lord Jesus Christ to those who do not know it, as an overflow of your life. When you walk in this peace, the peace of those around you will increase, although they carry turmoil. I bless you with being known as someone who carries the peace of God with you everywhere you go, so that people will seek you out because they are so desperate for the peace of God.

I bless you, _____, with being part of a community of faith that experiences the peace of God, that walks in a deep submission to the King of kings and Lord of lords and Prince of Peace—a fellowship that has learned to enthrone Jesus, so that their peace is pervasive, enough to bring peace to the world that is in darkness. I bless you with finding and connecting with others of like mind, so that in a community of faith your peace can be a part of that great light that shines out among a people who are in darkness. I bless you, _____, with an intimate relationship with God who makes peace. I bless you with that peace in the name of Jesus of Nazareth.

Respond with your spirit...
Write your thoughts, etc.

Day 10 Character

_____, I call your spirit to attention. Listen to the Word of God for you. "Grace and peace be yours in abundance through the knowledge of God and of Jesus our Lord. His divine power has given us everything we need for life and godliness through our knowledge of him who called us by his own glory and goodness. Through these he has given us his very great and precious promises, so that through them you may participate in the divine nature and escape the corruption in the world caused by evil desires. For this very reason, make every effort to add to your faith goodness; and to goodness, knowledge; and to knowledge, self-control; and to self-control, perseverance; and to perseverance, godliness; and to godliness, brotherly kindness; and to brotherly kindness, love. For if you possess these qualities in increasing measure, they will keep you from being ineffective and unproductive in your knowledge of our Lord Jesus Christ" (2 Peter 1:2-8).

> I SPEAK TO YOUR SLUMBERING SPIRIT TO WAKE UP, AND I SAY TO YOU THAT IT IS SAFE, IT IS TIME, IT IS RIGHT FOR YOUR SPIRIT TO LOOK OUTWARD AND UPWARD INTO THE FACE OF YOUR FATHER GOD.

_____, your Father designed your spirit, your soul, and your body, and He ordains and oversees their alignment. I call your spirit to the highest position in the name of Jesus Christ of Nazareth. I speak to your slumbering spirit to wake up, and I say to you that it is safe, it is time, it is right for your spirit to look outward and upward into the face of your Father God. Holy Spirit, come and speak to Your child's spirit the truth that he is accepted, affirmed, capable, and beloved in You, that he has no lack that detracts from who he is in Your eyes. Nothing can separate him from Your love. You like the way You made him. You are not intimidated by the areas that are lacking. You are perfectly sure of Your ability to heal those areas, to restore broken places, to finish his parenting. Holy Spirit, speak to his spirit in a language he can understand and receive. Your promise to him is that he has grace and peace in abundance in You, that as he pursues Jesus and knows Him more deeply, Your divine power gives him everything he needs for living a godly life and receiving his own glory and goodness.

_____, with your spirit hear the promise of your Father. Through His mighty power He has given you His very great and precious promises, so that through them you may share in the divine nature and escape the corruption in the world. In your spirit, receive these promises and the grace to pursue faith, goodness, knowledge, self-control, perseverance, godliness, brotherly kindness, and love. Receive the enabling power to live these qualities in increasing measure, so that you will not be ineffective or unproductive in knowing your Lord Jesus Christ.

I call your soul to attention, _____, saying, "Come under God's order; be healed, restored, and whole, submitted under your spirit. Be free from the spirit of fear that would paralyze you… fears for the future, fears of failure, fears of meaninglessness, fears of man, etc." I speak to your soul to discern the voice of your Father and your Savior who will never leave you or let you go and receive their love that casts out fear. Father, cut through the assaults of lies, soulishness, performance, religious spirits, all contrary words spoken or contrary prayers prayed, and everything that keeps your child's soul from being joyful, at peace, effective, and productive. _____, let your soul hear the Spirit of the Lord as never before, knowing you are in a safe place in your Father's house. He is pleased with the promises He has made to you, with your birthright, with your growth, with His work in progress in your life.

_____, I call your body to attention and command it to come into alignment with your spirit. Hormones, metabolic systems, immune system, wake/sleep control center, brain chemistry, and every physical system, listen to your Creator God who said, "This is very good" and gave His blessing when He made you. In Jesus' name, come into divine order and alignment with the awesome and wonderful way that God intended you to function— whole, healthy, well, strong, resilient, and alert. Come into alignment with the ordained order where God has placed you, because He determined the appointed times set for you and the exact places where you should live. Come into alignment with your Father God, the Creator of all things, the Ancient of Days, before creation, totally outside time. His covenant of life and peace and joy precedes and stands above all devices and snares of the enemy. I bless you, _____, with full participation in the divine nature, His covenants and His blessings, by His great and precious promises that He ratified in Jesus' death on the cross and sealed with the Holy Spirit resident in you. I bless you in the name of Jesus of Nazareth.

Respond with your spirit...

Write your thoughts, etc.

Day 11 Being Rescued

_____, I speak to your spirit in the name of Jesus of Nazareth. Listen with your spirit to the Word of God for you. "For in the day of trouble he will keep me safe in his dwelling; he will hide me in the shelter of his tabernacle and set me high upon a rock. Then my head will be exalted above the enemies who surround me; at his tabernacle will I sacrifice with shouts of joy; I will sing and make music to the Lord" (Psalm 27:5-6).

_____, there is a time for you to endure pain, knowing there is joy on the other side, a time for pressing on to get through the pain to enter into that joy. But there is also a time when you are supposed to be delivered by your Father, the Most High God, when you cry out to Him and ask Him to remove the obstacles, to lift you out of their clutches, and to set you in a beautiful, safe place. I bless you with knowing the difference between the two. I bless you with having the courage to move ahead and press through pain

I BLESS YOU WITH ENOUGH PROBLEMS IN LIFE AND GOD RESCUING YOU FROM THOSE PROBLEMS THAT YOU NO LONGER FEAR PROBLEMS BECAUSE THEY BECOME AN OPPORTUNITY FOR GOD TO SHOW HIMSELF STRONG.

when it is time. I bless you with freedom from a poverty spirit, with being willing and ready and knowing the time to cry out to your Father to be rescued from the problems that are not yours to fight. I bless you with seeing His provision in rescuing you in a multitude of ways. I bless you with enjoying the creativity of God in rescuing you, in little things and big things, monumental crises and little confusions of the day. I bless you with the joy of watching your Father easily handle those things that would perturb you or confuse you. I bless you with being rescued and celebrating His creativity in the rescue with the emotion of security.

I bless you with enough problems in life and God's rescuing you from those problems that you no longer fear problems because they become an opportunity for God to show Himself strong. I bless you with the blessing that Daniel had of living so long with God and experiencing His faithfulness so many times that when he was in the lions' den, he was not overwhelmed with fear. The animals' mouths were bound, and they could not bite him.

I bless you, _____, with the same security that David had, to walk into the enemy's camp and leave with Saul's spear and water bottle. I bless you with experiencing your Father's intervention so often and on such a profound level that you are emotionally secure. I bless you with seeing Him do remarkable things to rescue you, so that you can go before God's people and share glory stories of what God did on your behalf, and how He activated events to rescue you from the trap of the enemy designed to destroy you.

I bless you with the joy of imparting to other people the faith to walk in security. I bless you with stories of God's intervention that are so deeply woven into your spirit that sharing those stories with others lifts their faith up, lifts them out of fear, and enables them to have the faith to look forward and cry out for God's intervention in their own lives.

I bless you, _____, with the anointing that was upon Paul. The captain should not have set sail at that time and the ship was lost, but because Paul was on the ship, God kept everybody's life safe. I bless you with such an anointing of security that you will have the joy of God rescuing you, and also extending security to and rescuing others along with you. Your anointing for the powerful security of God will extend to those around you.

I bless you with the joy of your Father's acts on your behalf being translated into beautiful acts of worship toward Him. I bless you with not just enjoying the emotion of release and rescue, but also translating those experiences into acts of worship. I bless you with worshiping and glorifying God, encouraging His people, and memorializing His power after a magnificent rescue.

I bless you, _____, with shouts of joy over the intervening hand of God, as He rescues you from the work of His enemies and yours. I bless you with the security and joy of being rescued by the God whom you serve with all of your heart. I bless you in the name of Jesus of Nazareth.

Respond with your spirit...
Write your thoughts, etc.

Day 12 Obedience

_____, I call your spirit to attention in the name of Jesus of Nazareth. Listen with your spirit to the Word of God for you. "As the Father has loved me, so have I loved you. Now remain in my love. If you obey my commands, you will remain in my love, just as I have obeyed my Father's commands and remain in his love. I have told you this so that my joy may be in you and that your joy may be complete" (John 15:9-11).

_____, I bless you with the joy of obedience and with obedience being a joy, not a bondage. I bless you with the unique joy of obeying your Father in great detail because you are motivated by love. It is a terrible thing to obey because of fear that disobedience could cost you something, or to look at an authority and do what you need to do to avoid pain or punishment. It is beautiful when you obey God because you know it brings pleasure to Him, and you experience pleasure in experiencing the joy and love of your Father.

I bless you with seeing in the natural the results of your obedience. I bless you with understanding natural law, the universal cause-and-effect relationships that God has installed in the world, and with finding tremendous joy in understanding the designs of nature, of relationships, of spiritual intimacy and power. I bless you with seeing how to weave these laws together in new ways to produce new results.

I bless you, _____, with discovering hidden truths in Scripture. I bless you with the immense joy of first-fruits investments in these truths you discover, quickly seeing the fruit in your own life and the lives of others and celebrating the liberating power of God's truth. I bless you with having people bring to you problems that direct you to the Word of God. I bless you with eyes to see the biographies of Scripture and to mine out of those biographies rich understanding to see where they are reaping generational blessings and where they are reaping the results of God's law. I bless you with eyes to see the joy of obeying God's truth.

I bless you with experiencing the rich love of your Father as you are obeying Him. I bless you with seeing, hearing, and knowing the pleasure of your Father when you demonstrate your love for Him by your love for His commandments. Each level of your obedience will release a new level of your Father's joy to you. When you obey His law, your Father will celebrate you. I bless your spiritual ears and your spiritual eyes, the eyes of your understanding, to be open and to know the love of your Father, so that this will become the driving motivation to obey more and more.

I bless you with setting the standard of obedience in your community. Make it your spiritual ambition to be known as a person who loves the Lord and who is loved by the Lord. I bless your place in the new generation who will blot out the old stigma of legalism, because the world will see in your life the complete merging of obedience and love. I pray that as you celebrate all that your Father has for you, you will relish His love and that will be your mark in your community. I bless you

> I BLESS YOU WITH SEEING IN THE NATURAL THE RESULTS OF YOUR OBEDIENCE.

with obedience that leads you to that level of love and that level of love that leads you to obedience. Just as it says in the passage from John 15, "As the Father has loved me, so I have loved you, so remain in my love. If you obey my commands, you will remain in my love just as I remain in my Father's commands and remain in his love. I have told you this so that my joy may be in you and your joy may be complete."

33

_____, I bless you with complete joy, with discovering areas of obedience that will bring greater levels of joy, as you experience more of your Father's love resting upon you. I bless you in the name of Jesus of Nazareth.

Respond with your spirit...

Write your thoughts, etc.

Day 13 Mentoring

_____, I speak to your spirit in the name of Jesus of Nazareth. Listen with your spirit to the Word of God for you. "All your sons will be taught by the Lord, and great will be your children's peace" (Isaiah 54:13).

I bless you, _____, with knowing with certainty that you are your Father's beloved child, and that He knows you and the details of your identity. God knows everything He placed in you, and I bless you with being tutored and nurtured by the Most High God, like an apprentice learning a craft, not just information. I bless you as He develops and completes your identity, and you experience the presence of God and fulfillment of your birthright because of His presence in your life. The Lord wants to mentor you and coach you in being like Christ. I bless you with receiving that kind of deposit. I bless you with knowing that the Lord's hands are on all the circumstances of your life, so that every situation becomes a learning opportunity, as His Spirit guides you and equips you.

> ... I BLESS YOU WITH BEING TUTORED AND NURTURED BY THE MOST HIGH GOD...

I bless you, _____, with developing each part of your being so that you walk in wholeness, not only overcoming brokenness, but bringing all your gifts to full fruition. I bless you with knowing what your Father designed you to do and how He wants to use your gifts in accomplishing that work with humility and authenticity.

I bless you with a generational anointing of great peace because you are nurtured and mentored by the Lord of Peace Himself. You will need harmony between your giftings and the people in your world. I bless you with wholeness, fulfillment, reconciliation, and harmony in your relationships with other people. I bless you with richness in receiving into your life from other people's giftings, and I bless you with contributing to bringing peace to other people. I bless you with learning from the Lord Most High how to rebuild broken relationships. He has been rebuilding broken relationships throughout the history of mankind. I bless you with the Lord's anointing and skill as the greatest restorer of relationships. I bless you with establishing life-giving, full, harmonious relationships.

Should there be people who do not embrace who you are, the Lord will teach you when to stay in a time of rejection and when to move on and go to a new place. God is able to work both where there is a season of rejection and where there is acceptance. I bless you with being led by the Lord to know when to stay and when to go, so that you will have great peace with Him.

I bless you, _____, with completeness in your giftings. I bless your spirit; I bless your soul. I bless your body with peace, and I bless your life's work with fulfillment, harmony, and wholeness in the name of Jesus of Nazareth, who is perfect peace.

Respond with your spirit...
Write your thoughts, etc.

Day 14 Walking in Favor

_____, I say to your spirit to listen to the Word
of God for you. "For seven days they celebrated with joy
the Feast of Unleavened Bread, because the Lord had
filled them with joy by changing the attitude of the king of
Assyria, so that he assisted them in the work on the house
of God, the God of Israel" (Ezra 6:22).

_____, I bless you with the joy of having favor
in the eyes of others, both in the household of faith and
with non-Christians. I bless you with people who will come
alongside you, eager to help you in the work of the Lord
that He has appointed for you. I bless you with knowing
people who will help make you successful, who will believe
in you, and who will be encouraging and life-giving to you,
people who will propel you along in your life, taking the
initiative to serve you and your vision.

I bless you, _____, with the same kind of
restorative authority that Ezra had. I bless you with having
favor in resources. Because you are called to God's work in
God's way in God's time, you will experience the favor of
believers and unbelievers providing the resources necessary
to accomplish the work that God has for you. I bless you
with people who will make the road smooth before you
and find ways to serve you and invest in you and bless
you with time, attention, talent, practical assistance, and
treasure of all kinds. I bless you with having favor with
people who were previously enemies of Christ and the
cross, just as the king of Persia changed his mind, releasing
the captives of Israel to go back to their homeland. He
blessed them with freedom, all the temple treasures, a large
offering from among the Gentile nobility, tax exemption,
and a tremendous amount of resources. A king who did
not care about their God was moved by God to give them
tremendous favor. I bless you with favor with bureaucrats

and authorities, favor in the marketplace, favor as you come in and go out, favor in unexpected places. I bless you with experiencing God turn toward you those who are indifferent to or opposed to the things of God.

I bless you with favor in rebuilding and restoring the community around you, as the secular leadership, religious leadership, and civil government become aware that they do not have answers or wisdom to heal the brokenness of the culture. I bless you with the favor of God upon you so that those who are wounded and hurting in business, politics, church, and professional or social leadership will look upon you with favor, turn to you, and find the wisdom of God through you.

I bless you, _____, with having favor that is not poisoned by jealousy, that when you receive favor others will not covet what you have, but they will honor you and affirm that it is right, good, and proper, and there will be blessing for the favor you receive. I bless you with receiving favor from relationships and the culture around you to do what you were born to do. I bless you in the name of Jesus of Nazareth.

Respond with your spirit...

Write your thoughts, etc.

Day 15 Solving Problems

_____, I call your spirit to attention in the name of Jesus of Nazareth. Listen with your spirit to the Word of God for you. "Consider it pure joy, my brothers, whenever you face trials of many kinds" (James 1:2). "His intent was that now, through the church, the manifold wisdom of God should be made known to the rulers and authorities in the heavenly realms, according to his eternal purpose which he accomplished in Christ Jesus our Lord" (Ephesians 3:10-11).

_____, your culture centers around avoiding problems and greatly values happiness, which is defined as having others take care of your problems. That is a delusion. God placed Adam and Eve in the Garden in a perfect environment and a perfect relationship with Himself. Yet He created a problem for them: to take the resources of the Garden and the resources of their relationship with Him to the rest of the world and to subdue it.

> THE PROBLEMS GOD HAS DESIGNED FOR YOU TO SOLVE WILL BRING THE GREATEST TREASURES IN YOUR LIFE.

You were designed by your Father to face problems and solve them, not just to escape them. The problems God has designed for you to solve will bring the greatest treasures in your life. People are remembered for the problems they solve or the problems they create. I bless you with being remembered for the problems you solve. I bless you with wisdom and pure joy when you face different kinds of problems. Whatever problem you face, I bless you with rejoicing in the situation, instead of complaining and turning back.

_____, I bless you with the faith to look at problems through your Father's eyes and realize that every problem He brings you is an opportunity to experience His faithfulness. Ephesians 3:10-11 assumes that many colors of problems will make known the many different colors of God's wisdom to the rulers and authorities in the heavenly realms. God has an infinite amount of wisdom, and there are colors of God's wisdom that you do not yet know. He will position you so that He can bring new problems into your life, and you can reach deep into your Father's wisdom and find His multi-faceted wisdom to solve the problems that He brings you. When you do that, God releases through your life a color of wisdom that you have never seen. God will gain great glory, and the evil rulers and authorities in the heavenly realms will suffer great loss and great grief. Problems are the playing field for the wisdom of God to be displayed. There is a time and place for God to display His favor, for Him to lift you up out of a tight spot, to rescue you, to lift you to a safe place above your enemies. There is a time and place for God to give you favor in the eyes of people who should be your enemies. But there is a greater joy than either of those—that is the joy of discovering God's wisdom that flows in solving problems.

I bless you with not having a welfare spirit within you, so that you do not look to someone else to solve your problems, but that you rejoice in accordance with the Word of God and consider it a joy to receive from the hand of God new and different-colored problems, and you will search out the wisdom of God to solve those problems.

I bless you, _____, with rising to the challenge of finding wisdom. I bless you with the perseverance to dig in the Word of God, as if you are looking for gold and silver and jewels. You have to move a lot of dirt to find a few jewels, but their value is worth the effort. I bless you with the endurance to press on, to study and to look, to find those jewels of wisdom that will reveal new things of the nature of God. I bless you with perseverance to seek out the solutions.

I bless you with refusing to develop a theology of failure, never settling for something that is a contradiction of Scripture. I bless you with not buying into the enemy's lies to settle for an armed truce rather than real victory. I bless you with perseverance to spend decades if necessary, searching the Word of God and the mind of your Father to know the truths that will set you free and set other people free.

I bless you, _____, with having the mind of Christ, so that you can see things from His perspective and see solutions that others can't see. I bless you with wisdom to embrace God's painful solutions to problems. I bless you with the anointing of Mary of Bethany who received the truth that the crucifixion of Jesus Christ

I BLESS YOU WITH AN EXPERIENTIAL KNOWLEDGE OF GOD'S PRESENCE...

was imminent and it was good. May you have the wisdom of God to embrace His solutions, although they may seem bizarre or painful, and nobody has ever walked that way before.

I bless you, _____, with a trail-blazing anointing, to do things that have never been done before, revealing the wisdom of God, and in that anointing to have the great joy reserved for those willing to embrace pain. I bless you with the joy of fulfillment which is not available to those who are merely trying to be happy. I bless you with the joy of discovering the wisdom of God and the mind of Christ to solve problems. I bless you with His joy in the name of Jesus of Nazareth.

Respond with your spirit...

Write your thoughts, etc.

Day 16 Freedom from the Fear of Man

_____, I call your spirit to attention in the name of Jesus of Nazareth. Listen to the Word of God for you. "But the Lord said to him, 'Peace! Do not be afraid. You are not going to die.' So Gideon built an altar to the Lord there and called it 'The Lord is Peace'..." (Judges 6:23-24).

I bless you, _____, with freedom from the fear of man and from an unhealthy fear of God. I bless you with being like Gideon, seeing and experiencing the presence of God in the middle of a crisis situation. I bless you with having current experiences of God's presence, provision, and intervention. I bless you with not having to go back to prior generations to share glory stories of God's intervention. I bless you with your own stories. I bless you with an experiential knowledge of God's presence, His provision, His answer to your prayers, His solving your problems, His intervention in your life, so that although the enemy may be in the land and things are not going well, there is a rock-solid knowledge that your Father God is present, contemporary, and current in your culture, life, and circumstances.

I bless you with going to the Word of God and seeing specific promises your Father has made to you, being able to stand on those promises and savoring the joy, the security, and the excitement that comes when your Father answers your prayers based on His specific promises. Gideon saw himself as a survivor in a hostile environment, but God saw him as a mighty warrior, one who would free the entire nation from the Midianite invasion. When Gideon accepted that identity, he began to experience peace.

I bless you, _____, with the profound truth of knowing who you are. I bless you with having peace based on your identity in your Father's provision, protection, and purposes. I bless you with embracing your identity and realizing that when God calls you to battle, He will be there with you and for you, and your victory will lie in His hand, not in your expertise or resources. I bless you with knowing who you are called to be in the eyes of God. I bless you with experiencing beyond a shadow of doubt God's pleasure in you and who you are and how He sees you now and tomorrow. I bless you with the peace that comes in knowing who you are and that you are doing what your Father wants you to do, and that He is pleased with you. I bless you with the blessing of savoring, soaking in, and rejoicing in the protection of doing the right thing at the right time at the right place in the right way, because you know your identity in your Father's house. I bless your spirit with peace in the name of Jesus of Nazareth, who designed your identity.

Respond with your spirit...

Write your thoughts, etc.

Day 17 Life-giving Leadership

_____, in the name of Jesus of Nazareth, listen with your spirit to the Word of God for you. "Mordecai the Jew was second in rank to King Xerxes, preeminent among the Jews, and held in high esteem by his many fellow Jews, because he worked for the good of his people and spoke up for the welfare of all the Jews" (Esther 10:3).

Remember, _____, that peace is largely found in completeness and wholeness, which necessitates relationships. It is a blessing to have a life-giving leader. I bless you, _____, with many life-giving leaders and with experiencing different flavors of wisdom that come from different men and women. I bless you with having a variety of life-giving leaders so they can equip you and prepare you for the days to come. I bless you with leaders who give life by showing you favor and opening doors for you. I also bless you with leaders who give life by being firm in requiring you to learn disciplines and demonstrate diligence.

I bless you, _____, with life-giving leaders who minister to your spirit and bring you into a deep knowledge of the Most High God. I bless you with life-giving leaders who teach you to love the Word of God, who lead you to meditate on the Word of God so that your wisdom continually grows. I bless you with life-giving leaders who will teach you how to relate to other people, who model for you the joys of relationship and bring you into a high level of celebration in your family and your community of faith, where people live together in unity and experience anointing from God. I bless you with life-giving leaders in difficult times who can make a path for you where there seems to be no way. I bless you with life-giving leaders who give you perspective in difficult situations.

I bless you, _____, with a spirit that takes advantage of the blessings of life-giving leadership and learns from them so that you in turn will become a life-giving leader, so that you in your generation will widen and deepen the stream of generational blessings from which your natural children and spiritual children will draw. I bless you with far greater skill than your parents. I bless you with learning how to minister to your children in a wiser, richer way. I bless you with a good husband or a good wife. I bless you with bringing wholeness and life-giving skills into your marriage, so that you as a couple can bring the kingdom of God to bear on the society around you.

I bless you, _____, with being a leader in your community of faith so that other people spontaneously come to you when they have needs. I bless you to be a wise life-giver, not an enabler who inappropriately meets needs that people should take care of for themselves. I bless you with having a huge reservoir of peace within you, so that when you speak blessings of peace, peace becomes a reality in the lives of others. I bless you with an anointing on your speech so that you can speak peace to those around you.

I BLESS YOU WITH MEN AND WOMEN WHO COME ALONGSIDE YOU, INTERESTED IN THE HARVEST OF RIGHTEOUSNESS AND NOT IN THEIR OWN AGENDAS.

I bless you with being such a life-giving leader that you are welcomed into a community that has been hostile to you. I pray for such an anointing of wisdom and life-giving and peace upon you that you will be sought out and placed in positions of influence so that your life-giving may flow out from you like a river and peace may envelop the social settings where God places you.

I bless you, _____, with life-giving leaders to mentor you throughout your life, and I bless you with becoming a life-giving leader who blesses the next generation with life-giving mentoring. I bless you in the name of Jesus of Nazareth.

Respond with your spirit...

Write your thoughts, etc.

Day 18 Team of Peacemakers

_____, listen with your spirit to the Word of God, in the name of Jesus of Nazareth. "Peacemakers who sow in peace raise a harvest of righteousness" (James 3:18). "Two are better than one, because they have a good return for their work" (Ecclesiastes 4:9). "So the Lord stirred up the spirit of Zerubbabel son of Shealtiel, governor of Judah, and the spirit of Joshua son of Jehozadak, the high priest, and the spirit of the whole remnant of the people. They came and began to work on the house of the Lord Almighty, their God" (Haggai 1:14).

_____, it is good to be a peacemaker, but it is even better to be part of a team of peacemakers. Two are better than one. Two peacemakers working together can accomplish more than the two working individually. I bless you with being a peacemaker, and with your Father blessing you with additional peacemakers who work together with you to raise a harvest of righteousness. I bless you with men and women who come alongside you, interested in the harvest of righteousness and not in their own agendas. I bless you with men and women who have in themselves that wholeness, completeness, harmony of all their parts that they are at peace, so they are able to bring the harmony of their peace alongside yours. Together you can create a richer, fuller harmony to produce righteousness. I bless you with rare people of that caliber, brought into partnership with you.

I bless you as in Haggai 1:14, where the Lord stirred up the spirit of the governor, the high priest, and the whole remnant of the people. I bless you with your Father's stirring up the spirit of those whom He handpicks in positions of leadership, business, civil government, church, and even peers. These men and women of peace who look outside themselves will come to you and partner with you, so that you can sow in peace and raise a mighty harvest of righteousness.

I bless you, _____, with people who are seeking to grow other people and bring them into fullness and completeness, to a state of righteousness and harmony. I bless you with people who are not looking primarily to fix circumstances so they can walk in greater ease; rather, their internal peace will be the objective they are trying to replicate in the lives of others. I bless you with a multiplied harvest of righteousness in lives, in communities of faith, and in your culture. May God bless you with men and women who walk alongside you shoulder to shoulder, in harmony, without competition, without control, without manipulation, without contention. As a team you can reap a harvest of righteousness that will leave a verifiable, measurable, sustained imprint on the community around you. I bless you in the name of Jesus of Nazareth, who had a team of peacemakers with Him and who left an incredible harvest of righteousness behind Him.

Respond with your spirit...
Write your thoughts, etc.

Day 19 Friends During Transition and Change

_____, in the name of Jesus of Nazareth listen with your spirit to the Word of God for you. "Other Benjamites and some men from Judah also came to David in his stronghold. David went out to meet them and said to them, 'If you have come to me in peace, to help me, I am ready to have you unite with me. But if you have come to betray me to my enemies when my hands are free from violence, may the God of our fathers see it and judge you.' Then the Spirit came upon Amasai, chief of the Thirty, and he said: 'We are yours, O David! We are with you, O son of Jesse! Success, success to you, and success to those who help you, for your God will help you.' So David received them and made them leaders of his raiding bands" (1 Chronicles 12:16-18).

> ...YOU ARE LIVING IN A TIME WHEN CHANGE FROM GOD'S OLD ORDER TO GOD'S NEW ORDER IS HAPPENING AT A FASTER PACE THAN EVER BEFORE.

God had established Saul as king over Israel, but God later determined to end his reign. David was chosen, appointed, anointed, loved by God, but he was not yet king because Saul was still on the throne. Saul knew that God had chosen David to be the next king, that the favor of God had departed from him and was resting on David, and Saul bitterly resented God's changing the structure. One of the most difficult changes is from God's order to God's new order. God chose and anointed Saul for that season, God's order for a time, but that time passed. God had a new order, a dynasty headed by King David. For the new order to be put in place, the old order had to be removed. In the transition, there was a lot of pain and turmoil. Saul was trying to kill the appointed king of the new order.

Into this time of crisis and human resistance to the divine new order, God brought men to David to be at peace with him, support him, encourage him, stand alongside him, as he moved through the tumultuous passage from God's order to God's new order. Some of these men were Benjamites from the same tribe as Saul. They should have been loyal to Saul, yet they were men of vision and conviction who set aside the human loyalties of tribe and saw the benefits of the new order clearly. Men of Judah did not side with David initially, but they began to see that God's new order was resting with him. They chose to leave their homes, the security of their cities, the favor of the king of the old order. They came to the desert to experience privation, need, hardship, instability, transition, hatred by the old order. It greatly encouraged David to have these men come to him during the time of transition. Many came to him after the new order was established, but men of faith and courage came to him during the time of transition from God's old order to God's new order. God used these men in later years to be the leaders of Israel. David and his mighty men established authority and dominion over all of Israel after he became king.

> THE ENEMY WILL DO EVERYTHING POSSIBLE TO MAGNIFY THE PAIN AND CAUSE YOU TO FOCUS ON THE PAIN, BUT I BLESS YOU WITH AN AWARENESS OF THE JOY SET BEFORE YOU.

_____, you are living in a time when change from God's old order to God's new order is happening at a faster pace than ever before. More new things are being brought into the stream of world history than at any other time. There will be many changes, and you will be part of God's new order. You may be resented by God's old order, renounced and criticized. These things are inevitable. God did not protect David from those things, but he gave David peace during the transition by bringing to him men to walk alongside him.

I bless you, _____, with being in strong, rich, life-giving relationships with men and women who believe in God's new order, who understand that you are part of God's new order. I bless you with men and women of faith coming alongside you, committed to you personally for those days and times when God calls you to lead out in the transition from His old order to His new order. I bless you with having God's appointed leaders of His new order who walk beside you in unity in that difficult transition. I bless you with being a life-giving blessing to those people during the transition, mentoring those who have the faith to see that you are part of God's new order. When God's new order is established, you will have many standing with you, partnering with you. I bless you with a strong personal and corporate sense of His presence as His signature on your calling. I bless you in the name of Jesus of Nazareth, who himself led out in the transition between God's old order and God's new order.

Respond with your spirit...

Write your thoughts, etc.

Day 20 The Prize

_____, listen with your spirit to the Word of God for you. "Therefore, since we are surrounded by such a great cloud of witnesses, let us throw off everything that hinders and the sin that so easily entangles, and let us run with perseverance the race marked out for us. Let us fix our eyes on Jesus, the author and perfecter of our faith, who for the joy set before him endured the cross, scorning its shame, and sat down at the right hand of the throne of God" (Hebrews 12:1-2).

As much as you are loved, _____, you have experienced pain in your life. This world is under a curse, and you are part of a great battle against the enemy of Most High God. You will endure pain. I bless your spirit with the ability to have joy that transcends pain. I bless you with a clear picture of what is before you, the thing that God has called you to do, so that you can endure pain to get there. For the joy set before Him, Jesus Christ, the author and perfecter of your faith, endured the cross. He endured more pain than you ever will. He paid a higher price. He suffered greatly for you to receive these blessings. I bless you with having His joy set before you. You must have a clear view of what is on the other side of the pain. I bless you with eyes to see the joy set before you. The enemy will do everything possible to magnify the pain and cause you to focus on the pain, but I bless you with an awareness of the joy set before you. I bless you with stepping up to the battle for joy.

Listen again with your spirit to the Word of God. "Therefore, I urge you, brothers, in view of God's mercy, to offer your bodies as living sacrifices, holy and pleasing to God—this is your spiritual act of worship. Do not conform any longer to the pattern of this world, but be transformed by the renewing of your mind. Then you will be able to test and approve what God's will is—His good, pleasing, and perfect will" (Romans 12:1-2).

_____, I bless you with testing and approving what your Father's good, pleasing, and perfect will is. I bless you with discerning between the good and the best. I bless you with discerning the traps of the enemy, the false offers that he makes. I bless you with discerning between the real joy that your Father offers and a counterfeit, transitory joy that the enemy offers. I bless you with an understanding from the Word of God to receive the principles of his Word and the joy that you can expect. I bless you with hearing through revelation from the Spirit things that are specific to your own life, so that you can savor in your spirit the joy set before you. I bless you with rejoicing in the knowledge of God's will as He reveals it, for He cannot reveal to you now everything that is on His heart. I bless you with receiving all the joy that God wants to show you.

> THE WORLD OFFERS YOU HAPPINESS, SATAN OFFERS YOU DELUSION, BUT GOD OFFERS YOU THE JOY OF HIS PRESENCE THAT COMES FROM PARTNERING WITH HIM.

Listen again with your spirit to God's Word. "I have much more to say to you, more than you can now bear. But when he, the Spirit of truth, comes, he will guide you into all truth. He will not speak on his own; he will speak only what he hears, and he will tell you what is yet to come" (John 16:12-13).

I bless you, _____, with receiving every new revelation that the Spirit of God gives you, to see clearly each facet of joy that your Father is offering you. The world offers you happiness, Satan offers you delusion, but God offers you the joy of His presence that comes from partnering with Him. I bless you with embracing the call of God for each chapter of your life, seeing His joy in each step of your life, so that you advance to the next revelation and the next. I bless you with sufficient understanding of the joy set before you that you will not count the cost, but you will pay the price.

I bless you with godly dissatisfaction, that you will always hunger and thirst for new joys, new levels of your Father's revealing His joy to you. I bless you with joy beyond any joys you have already experienced. I bless you with possessing your birthright in full, with never being satisfied with a single measure of joy, but with always wanting more, wanting the very best God has for you. I bless you with yearning for the fullness of joy that is beyond what you have already experienced, so that you embrace any pain, scorn the shame, and pay the price to possess your birthright.

I bless you with a profound, deep, driving desire for more of the joy that you have a legal right to have, joy that is coupled to your birthright. I bless you with hunger for more joy and for the satisfaction of that hunger. I bless you, in the name of Jesus of Nazareth.

Respond with your spirit...
Write your thoughts, etc.

Day 21 Knowing the Peace of Jesus

_____, listen with your spirit to the Word of God for you. "Peace I leave with you; my peace I give you. I do not give to you as the world gives. Do not let your hearts be troubled and do not be afraid" (John 14:27).

Jesus gave His peace to the disciples before He left His earthly relationship with them and returned to heaven. His peace which was transferred to them had various aspects. First there was a profound relationship with His Father which gave Him legitimacy in everything He did. It did not matter to Jesus that other people did not understand Him or that they opposed Him. None of that affected His absolute certainty of who He was and His significance, because He had a relationship with His Father. He knew what His Father wanted Him to do, and He did it. There was nothing that could damage His relationship with His Father.

So, _____, I bless you with that kind of peace. I bless you with knowing deep in your spirit that God your Father's favor is upon you, that He loves you, likes you, enjoys you, and takes pleasure in who you are today, regardless of what you do. He finds pleasure in you while you sleep and when you wake up. I bless you with profoundly knowing that reality. I bless you with knowing your Father's love, with being secure, and having the peace of Jesus in your relationship with your Father.

Another aspect of Jesus' relationship with his Father was that He had a sense of being adequate for the task at hand. He was prepared and trained by His Father. There were different seasons of His life: times of immense pain and of intense pleasure, and times of loneliness and of friendship. Yet whatever He faced, He went into each day knowing that with His Father partnering with Him, He was adequate for the task to which His Father called Him. There was no anxiety, no fear, no sense that God would put Him in a place without giving Him the resources to meet the day.

So, _____, I bless you with that same sense of adequacy. I bless you with the assurance that each day will be Father-filtered, that God Himself will see to it that nothing comes into your life that is beyond what His strength in you can handle. I bless you with the peace of knowing ahead of time that your Father God will partner with you to provide adequacy for each day, whether it is a day filled with pain or with pleasure.

A third aspect of Jesus' peace was that He knew what His Father wanted Him to do. He knew what His Father was doing from the beginning of time, and He did the same works that His Father was doing.

So, _____, I bless you with knowing in your spirit before you know in your mind the works of your Father. I bless you with understanding in your spirit what your Father has called you to do, with knowledge so clear and strong that nobody can dissuade you from what God has called you to do. I bless you with a clear sense of the call of God on your life: the big picture as well as a daily sense of what God would have you do.

A fourth aspect of the peace of Jesus was timing. At age 12 he eagerly desired to be about His Father's business, yet He recognized God's direction in telling Him to wait another 18 years. His heart yearned to be in ministry, yet He knew it wasn't time. When it was time, He was on time, and He was positioned for His baptism, for His first miracle, for each of the major events of His life, and even for His death, His resurrection, and His ascension. Every aspect of His life was on time. He did the right thing at the right time. He had a knowledge of timing and that gave Him peace.

I bless you, _____, with the peace Jesus had of being at the right place at the right time, of being able to live with urgency within Himself without being overwhelmed by that urgency, because He knew that His Father's time was right. I bless you with having a passion that burns within you, but I bless you with knowing God's perfect time for that fire to manifest in ministry.

Another aspect of Jesus' peace was His sense of perspective. He knew where the individual pieces fit into the big picture. Most people looked on His impending death on the cross as a terrible thing, but Jesus saw it in the scope of all of history, because He was the Lamb slain before the foundation of the world. He put pleasure in perspective and realized that those who worshiped Him today would be gone tomorrow. He put ministry in perspective, knowing that the seed He sowed today, although it was not well received, would bear fruit another day. He had an abiding peace because of His understanding of His Father's big picture.

I bless you, _____, with the peace that Jesus had which is beyond what the world gives. I bless you with greater understanding and larger perspective than most people have, and I bless you with the peace of Jesus in being able to undergo things in your life that you don't understand without a troubled heart, knowing that He holds the ultimate perspective. I bless you with the peace that Jesus has for you in the name of Jesus of Nazareth.

Respond with your spirit...
Write your thoughts, etc.

Day 22 Bringing the Glory of God

_____, listen with your spirit to the Word of God for you. "So David and the elders of Israel and the commanders of units of a thousand went to bring up the ark of the covenant of the Lord from the house of Obed-Edom, with rejoicing" (1 Chronicles 15:25).

The ark of the covenant was the mark of the manifest presence of God. The Philistines had captured the ark over 40 years before. David wanted to right this wrong and have the glory of God abiding in Jerusalem. With good intentions but flawed methodology, he took many people to bring the ark up to Jerusalem; however they made a mistake, and God killed one of the men. So they stopped and left the ark in the home of Obed-Edom. David later brought the ark up to Jerusalem correctly with great rejoicing.

_____, your culture is yearning and crying out for something more than religion or churchianity—it is crying out for the legitimate, powerful presence of God to move among His people. There is a great deal of mobilization to bring a new move of God. Flawed and inadequate methods have been disappointing and not looked upon with favor by God.

I bless you with a desperate hunger and thirst for bringing the manifest glory of God to your community. I bless you with the vision and anointing to see what is necessary to prepare the way, what God requires of you before He will come and tabernacle with you. I bless you with implementing the truth from the Word of God that will bring the joy of visitation of God into your family, or community, or city. I bless you with being the leader or having a leader with the anointing to implement the necessary components to do the job— the scribes and Levites who know the truth and the king who is in a position to organize everything and bring revival into

your community and your family. I bless you with having
favor with those who are a part of the gift mix for this to
happen—leaders, followers, the churched, and unchurched.

_____, I bless you with cutting a new path
without violating the old path. David was chosen by God
to introduce a new facet of worship into the stream of
religious history. For 500 years there was no worship with
music in the tabernacle. There were sights, sounds, smells,
ceremonies, clothing, and routines of worship that pleased
God, but no musical worship. God waited over 500 years
for His man to have the creativity to introduce music as
worship. David was that man. When David tried to bring up
the ark the first time, he had all kinds of musicians, but he
violated the way that God had prescribed that the ark would
be moved. In his excitement about embracing the new good
thing, he ignored the old, and God judged the process.
Later David stood on the foundation of the old and obeyed
the commands to carry the ark on staves on the shoulders
of the priests. He stood on the righteous foundation of the
past, without violating it, and then he added worship, the
new thing he wanted to introduce.

I bless you with the wisdom and anointing to stand
solidly on the righteous past, yet not be locked in to the
forms and manners of tradition. I bless you with seeing
outside the traditions and norms of the religious movement
into which you were born. I bless you with eyes to see the
new paths, to minister the new forms of serving God with
new songs. I bless you with the ability to sing the song of the
gospel in a different key, doing no violence to the Word or
the message that must remain unchanged. I bless you with
the blessing of David, to hold the truth of the old and bring
in the revelation of the new and to experience the manifest
presence of God in your community. I bless you in the
name of Jesus of Nazareth.

Respond with your spirit...

Write your thoughts, etc.

Day 23 Reproducing Your Values

_____, listen with your spirit to the Word of God for you. "I know, my God, that you test the heart and are pleased with integrity. All these things have I given willingly and with honest intent. And now I have seen with joy how willingly your people who are here have given to you. O Lord, God of our fathers Abraham, Isaac and Israel, keep this desire in the hearts of your people forever, and keep their hearts loyal to you" (1 Chronicles 29:17-18).

One of the core values of David was worshiping God in a magnificent way. He centered his life around different forms of worship. He desired to worship God by building a temple where He could dwell, but God told David that his son would build it. Willingly, with integrity, and with honest intent, he gave his personal treasures for the temple. He gave his efforts as king to assemble tremendous resources for the construction of the temple. He called together the leaders of the nation and invited them to give an offering. They gave an immense offering with the same willingness as David, not out of manipulation or pressure. They embraced his same value. As king, he had ruled so effectively that his value had captured the hearts of the leadership of the nation, so they gave generously, willingly, and with integrity of heart.

_____, I bless you with the joy of transferring your vision to the hearts and spirits of others. I bless you with building your vision and your values into your followers and seeing your vision and values replicated in others. I bless you with being the kind of leader who can imprint passion and values deep into the being of your followers. I bless you with the joy of seeing your followers in ministry embrace your values at the deepest level. I bless you with seeing your followers take what God has conceived in you, your vision, your passion, and live them out and implement them in multiplied ways that you have not. I bless you with seeing your spiritual grandchildren living out your values, those who have been mentored by people you have mentored. I bless you with the joy of seeing in your spiritual grandchildren and great-grandchildren deep, inner, heart-felt commitment to the values that God has placed in your heart, because God has also written it in their hearts.

_____, listen again with your spirit to the Word of God for you. "You became imitators of us and of the Lord" (1 Thessalonians 1:6).

I bless you with the joy of seeing your followers live the life of the Spirit that they absorb from you as they partner with you. I bless you to see them use the values that you have lived, modeled and instilled as a platform for them to embrace the ways of God at an even higher level and possess their birthrights. I bless you with beautifully imprinting God's heart on others and knowing that you have left an indelible imprint for good on the lives of many. I bless you as people embrace your values, people that you did not know were watching or learning from you, people to whom you were not overtly ministering. I bless you with the wonderful joy of seeing your values embraced by a wider circle than those whom you directly touched.

I bless you with great fulfillment and satisfaction at the end of your life, knowing that your family and generations that follow you have embraced your values as their values. I bless you extravagantly in the name of Jesus of Nazareth.

Respond with your spirit...

Write your thoughts, etc.

Day 24 Hunger for God

_____, listen with your spirit to the Word of God for you. "There was great joy in Jerusalem, for since the days of Solomon son of David king of Israel there had been nothing like this in Jerusalem. The priests and the Levites stood to bless the people, and God heard them, for their prayer reached heaven, his holy dwelling place" (2 Chronicles 30:26-27).

This passage deals with the revival under righteous King Hezekiah who lived about 300 years after David. The king directly before Hezekiah was an incredibly evil man, but Hezekiah's culture had heard of the great visitation of God in the past. They still sang the songs of David and his worshipers. They knew of the miracles of the past, but they had not experienced them in their lifetime. They found comfort in what God used to do, but they ached to see something more than the power of the idolatrous culture in which they were living at the time. The remnant knew what it was to be a hidden people in a crooked and perverse generation.

God moved in Hezekiah to begin a renewal by a deliberate and careful process, withstanding apathy and opposition. He cleansed the temple, the courtyard, then Jerusalem, then Judea, then all of Israel. He called for people who had not celebrated the Passover for a generation to sanctify themselves and come together to restore the righteous worship that God had instituted with Moses. The people responded with heartfelt passion and tremendous joy. They came together and celebrated in Jerusalem the greatest Passover that Israel had ever celebrated. Because there was an open heaven over them when the Levites prayed, God heard, and a torrent of blessings was released in the heavenlies upon His people, and there was great joy.

_____, the culture in which you live is like that of Hezekiah. Most of the culture is saturated with sin and iniquity. There is a continual release of depraved ideas and depraved leaders, leading people into deeper depravity, but there is an aching among righteous people, a hunger for a visitation of holy God. The stories of past visitations are selling very well, and fresh biographies have been written about great men of the past.

Part of the remnant today is still looking back, as in the day of Habakkuk. "Lord, I have heard of your fame; I stand in awe of your deeds, O Lord. Renew them in our day, in our time make them known; in wrath remember mercy" (Habakkuk 3:2). The remnant that is looking back knows what God has done, where He has been, and they are looking to see the past reoccur today. _____, God is not planning to reproduce the past in our generation. He is planning to do a new thing, and there is a hunger for a new move of God in our time. Whether it is a revival in your own family, or your community of faith, or your city, or your nation, I bless you with the joy of experiencing a visitation of the presence of God in your life.

I BLESS YOU WITH ENTERING INTO A COVENANT OF LIFE AND PEACE.

I bless you with seeing a new move of God. I bless you with the joy of experiencing a fresh taste of the presence and glory of your Father God in a decadent culture. I bless you with having a fresh manifestation of the glory and power of God in your day and in your time. I bless you with a powerful new move among righteous people who have deliberately and intentionally sought God, who have paid the price of doing the holy things that needed to be done, and of destroying the altars and idols of a culture that does not want them destroyed.

_____, I bless you with the passion for God that King Hezekiah had. I bless you with starting as a minority of one, like Hezekiah; very few religious leaders backed him when he first proposed returning to God. I bless you with having the intentionality and tenacity in your lifetime to multiply yourself, multiply the faith and the passion in your life into two, then four, then sixteen, then more. I bless you with igniting such a measure of hunger and holiness in your family, your community, and your nation that many will experience a visitation of God. I bless you with knowing about the past and knowing the hopes and prophecies about the future. In that bracket between yesterday and tomorrow, I bless you with the extravagant joy of being today's man and experiencing a visitation of God in a fresh way in your day and in your time. I bless you in the name of Jesus of Nazareth, Lord of the revived heart.

Respond with your spirit...

Write your thoughts, etc.

64

Day 25 Generational Covenant of Life and Peace

_____, listen with your spirit to God's Word for you. "My covenant was with [Levi], a covenant of life and peace, and I gave them to him; this called for reverence and he revered me and stood in awe of my name. True instruction was in his mouth and nothing false was found on his lips. He walked with me in peace and uprightness, and turned many from sin" (Malachi 2:5-6).

I BLESS YOU WITH WAKING UP EACH MORNING WITH AWE THAT GOD WOULD CHOOSE TO BE IN COVENANT WITH YOU, BECAUSE OUT OF THAT BLESSING OF AWE OF GOD WILL COME INSTRUCTION, WISDOM, AND WORDS OF TRUTH FROM YOUR LIPS.

God's original intent was that all twelve tribes would be priestly tribes, that they would be a nation of priests to the nations of the world. Due to sin in the camp, many of them lost that privilege, and Levi as a tribe was chosen to be the priestly tribe to represent the nation. God created a covenant of life and peace with that tribe. He gave them life and peace to give to others. Malachi says this called for reverence. God is inviting you to come into a covenant of life and peace with him. When you enter into that covenant, you receive a richer title than that of Levi. You become a member of the royal priesthood. You have received peace from God, and you are learning to walk in that peace and to bring others into that peace. This is foundational.

The next step is to have a reverential awe of God who reconciled you to Himself and gave you such a covenant of life and peace. Ponder the marvel and privilege of His covenant of life and peace with you, and God will place true instruction in your mouth. God's intent is that you will come to know Him more deeply, as you celebrate the majesty of what He has done for you in giving you this covenant of life and peace. It will unlock deeper and more profound truths from the Word of God, so that your lips will have an anointing for true instruction. The last step is that Levi turned many from sin, as he walked with God in peace and personal uprightness.

I bless you, _____, with this same anointing, although you walk in a different priesthood. I bless you with entering into a covenant of life and peace. I bless you with knowing your Father and speaking of Him and bringing many others to know Him. I bless you with an anointing of revering God that produces wisdom, so that true instruction comes from your mouth, being fruitful, life-giving, and transformational. I bless you with turning many from their sin and bringing many into the same reverence that you have of Most High God. The hardness and profound lack of reverence of your culture is an invitation for God to do bigger things for you than He has done in other generations. It has nothing to do with the hardness of the culture and everything to do with the anointing of God and His revelation.

I bless you, _____, with not taking for granted the anointing for reverence that you have in the covenant of life and peace. I bless you with waking up each morning with awe that God would choose to be in covenant with you, because out of that blessing of awe of God will come instruction, wisdom, and words of truth from your lips. I bless you with words of truth that are piercing, encouraging, and clarifying. I bless those words of instruction to be articulated in many ways. I bless you with the blessing that Samuel had, that "...none of his words fell to the ground" (1 Samuel 3:19). I bless you with words of instruction so anointed with the wisdom and reverence of God that you turn many from sin.

I bless you, _____, with a profound generational anointing of peace on your life that will bring reverence and wisdom to generations after you. I bless you that the family line you establish may be known as a family of peace, a family that imparts peace, a family of wisdom, of reverence, and of holiness. I bless you with bringing many in the next generation into reverence of God so that they have the wisdom of God. They in turn may turn many to a covenant of life and peace with God so that the next generation would revere God and have words of wisdom for the next generation after that. I bless you with laying the foundations for many godly generations through being in a covenant of life and peace with Most High God. I bless you with all these blessings of peace, in the name of the Prince of Peace, in the name of the God who makes peace, who instructs you and mentors you in peace, so that all your children and children's children will have great peace. I bless you in the name of Jesus of Nazareth.

Respond with your spirit...

Write your thoughts, etc.

Day 26 Destroying Authority that Establishes Chaos

_____, listen with your spirit to the Word of God for you. "Stand firm then, with the belt of truth buckled around your waist, with the breastplate of righteousness in place, and with your feet fitted with the readiness that comes from the gospel of peace. In addition to all this, take up the shield of faith, with which you can extinguish all the flaming arrows of the evil one. Take the helmet of salvation and the sword of the Spirit, which is the word of God. And pray in the Spirit on all occasions with all kinds of prayers and requests. With this in mind, be alert and always keep on praying for all the saints" (Ephesians 6:14-18).

This well-known portion of Scripture on spiritual warfare describes the armor of the believer. Look at the feet fitted with the readiness of the gospel of peace. Peace destroys the authority that establishes chaos. The enemy creates chaos through division and alienation. He fractures relationships, subtly or overtly, between man and God, between people in every facet of society, even in man's relationship with nature. We must war against the enemy who creates chaos and destroy his authority to establish chaos. To have authority against the demonic structure that establishes chaos, we must live a lifestyle of being peacemakers, of knowing how to bring the peace of God to bear on the fragmentation of our culture. Jesus modeled this. At times He was assertive; at times He was compassionate. At times He forgave the most overt sinner, and at times He confronted the seemingly "righteous" religious structure. Jesus used different tools to destroy the authority structures that bring chaos.

I bless you, _____, with being a student of the peacemaking skills of Jesus Christ. I bless you with having ears to hear what the Spirit is saying to your spirit, and I bless you with improving your skill of hearing your

Father's voice. I bless you with being led by your Father in situations where there is chaos, division, and alienation, so that you have opportunity often to practice the art of being a peacemaker. I bless you with well-fitted shoes on your feet that are ready to bring the gospel of peace in all of its different colors and forms upon a multitude of situations around you. Jesus said, "Blessed are the peacemakers, for they will be called sons of God" (Matthew 5:9). I bless you to aspire to that title, that you would be called a son of God because you have mastered the art of being a peacemaker. I bless you to destroy the spiritual structure that authorizes chaos in every situation where people don't want peace, where people are turning against you and the things of God. God will bring you into a multitude of situations like that, for this world is full of chaos, brokenness, and alienation. The structures of the enemy are everywhere. I bless you with endurance in peace-making, because being a peacemaker is a difficult thing.

_____, I bless you with honing your peace-making skills as He takes you through one apprenticeship after another, grooming you to wear the title of peacemaker, as a son of God. I bless you with being a peacemaker who has the spiritual authority to demolish the strongholds which bring chaos into your family and your community. I bless you with setting your face like flint toward the goal of being a peacemaker and being sought out because you have high authority over the spiritual structures that bring chaos. I bless you with having your feet shod with a readiness that comes from the gospel of peace. I bless you with being one of the sons of God, in the name of Jesus of Nazareth, who was your prototype.

Respond with your spirit...

Write your thoughts, etc.

Day 27 Friendship During Pruning

_____, listen with your spirit to the Word of God for you. "Jonathan said to David, 'Go in peace, for we have sworn friendship with each other in the name of the Lord, saying, "The Lord is witness between you and me, and between your descendants and my descendants forever."' Then David left, and Jonathan went back to the town" (1 Samuel 20:42).

You will go through seasons of pruning, when your Father removes from you good things—friendships, privilege, ministry platform, money, sustenance, hope, even your reputation. Pruning is always very painful and very difficult, although you may have a clear conscience and know that it comes from God, and that there are promises of a better and more fruitful future. It usually results in being very much alone. Most people will shy away from you when you experience pain. David was blessed to have one friend who stood solidly with him through God's pruning. Six hundred friends stood with him and walked with him through the pruning season and into the season of abundance.

> I BLESS YOU WITH THE RIGHT AMOUNT OF PRUNING IN THE RIGHT SEASONS OF YOUR LIFE FOR REDEMPTIVE ETERNAL PURPOSES.

I bless you, _____, with the prunings of the Lord. As painful as they are, they are for the best. They come from your wise Father. I bless you with the right amount of pruning in the right seasons of your life for redemptive eternal purposes.

I bless you with deep, solid life-giving friendships when you are going through a season of God's pruning you. I bless you with friendships that are designed, crafted, nurtured, and given to you by your Father, even at the same time that He is taking away other friendships that you have deemed important and necessary to your life. Although you may be severely pruned, I bless you with at least one friend who maintains covenant relationship with you in your darkest hour and is able to encourage you, strengthen you, and focus your attention on your Father's promises.

I bless you with additional friendships with people who come alongside you in the desert times. May they walk with you, encourage you, war with you, seek God's will with you, and wait with you. I bless you with friends who understand God's ways, but who can walk with you even when they don't understand His ways. I bless you with encouraging love that reminds you of the love that your Father has for you. I bless you with these things in the name of Jesus of Nazareth.

Respond with your spirit...

Write your thoughts, etc.

Day 28 An Ambassador of Peace
Sent to Reconcile

_____, listen with your spirit to the Word of God for you. "As it is written: 'There is no one righteous, not even one; there is no one who understands, no one who seeks God. All have turned away, they have together become worthless; there is no one who does good, not even one. Their throats are open graves; their tongues practice deceit. The poison of vipers is on their lips. Their mouths are full of cursing and bitterness. Their feet are swift to shed blood; ruin and misery mark their ways, and the way of peace they do not know. There is no fear of God before their eyes'" (Romans 3:10-18). "How, then, can they call on the one they have not believed in? And how can they believe in the one of whom they have not heard? And how can they hear without someone preaching to them? And how can they preach unless they are sent? As it is written, 'How beautiful are the feet of those who bring good news!'" (Romans 10:14-15)

I BLESS YOU WITH FINDING A WAY TO EXPRESS THE MUSIC OF THE GOSPEL TO THOSE WHO HAVE REJECTED THE SONG MANY TIMES BEFORE AND HAVE NEVER REALLY HEARD IT WITH THEIR SPIRIT, BY PRESENTING IT IN NEW KEYS AND NEW RHYTHMS.

All around you in your culture, there is so much iniquity, brokenness, rejection of God. So many people with no peace within themselves are wounding other people. When someone has no peace within, they take away the peace of others around them. People who have no peace need someone to tell them about the salvation of Jesus Christ and that they are designed by God to do beautiful, holy, wonderful things with the power of God working through them.

_____, I bless you with being one of those who is sent to go to people who lack peace, to take the peace that is within you and share it with them. I bless you with being sent to clearly express the good news of the gospel story in ways that it has never been told before, as well as in timeless ways as it has been told many times. I bless you with finding a way to express the music of the gospel to those who have rejected the song many times before and have never really heard it with their spirits, to be able to present it in new keys and new rhythms. I bless you with an anointing in your spirit to open closed doors of other people's spirits, so that the message of the gospel might speak from your spirit to their spirit, confirmed by the Holy Spirit of the true and living God. Their closed minds will be no barrier to the sound of freedom that comes from your lips to their spirits. I bless you with the Spirit of God working in the heart and spirit of those who hear, so that they can believe.

_____, I bless you with an anointing of faith that goes along with your anointing of peace to evangelize. I bless you so that whether you are speaking one-on-one or publicly to hundreds, faith will be imparted through your life to the spirit of the listener. May they have faith to believe the incomprehensible story of the gospel of Jesus' death and resurrection, providing reconciliation with God and man and peace for them. I bless you to encourage them to act upon that faith, to embrace the message they have heard and be converted.

I bless you with the beautiful feet of one who brings good news to a wounded, broken generation that has rejected many forms of Christianity but has not truly known Christ who brings peace. I bless you with profound reconciliation with God that leads to fearless compulsion to share the peace that you have with others. I bless you with opportunities that come to you because of the peace with

God that you have received, having been made whole, all the parts of your identity coming into completeness and harmony. I bless you with peace that emanates from you because of these things, causing people to seek you out and ask you about the hope that is within you. I bless you with evangelism's being a natural and normal part of your life, the normal conversation that you have with strangers and friends alike. I bless you with a vast harvest in your generation of family, of friends, of strangers you meet in passing. I bless you with having the beautiful feet of one who brings good news in such a way that people hear, understand, believe, and receive the reconciliation Jesus purchased with His own blood. I bless you with being a mighty reconciler, bringing people into peace with God. I bless you in the name of Jesus of Nazareth, the Prince of Peace.

Respond with your spirit...

Write your thoughts, etc.

Day 29 Used by God to Turn the Enemy's Plans Upside Down

_____, listen with your spirit to the Word of God for you. "Mordecai recorded these events, and he sent letters to all the Jews throughout the provinces of King Xerxes, near and far, to have them celebrate annually the fourteenth and fifteenth days of the month of Adar as the time when the Jews got relief from their enemies, and as the month when their sorrow was turned into joy and their mourning into a day of celebration. He wrote them to observe the days as days of feasting and joy and giving presents of food to one another and gifts to the poor" (Esther 9:20-22). "And having disarmed the powers and authorities, he made a public spectacle of them, triumphing over them by the cross" (Colossians 2:15).

When the Jews were in captivity, an evil man named Haman tried to destroy the nation of the Jews. He got the authority of the king by deception. He passed laws directing the killing of the Jews. God moved in a powerful way to save the Jews and to secure their peace and prosperity within an enemy people. Mordecai ordained two days of celebration after their sorrow was turned into joy. When Jesus was on the cross, He appeared to be losing everything. Yet His death on the cross paid the penalty for your sins and mine. Therefore, Satan has no more legal right over us once we confess our sins and claim the salvation and protection that our Father offers us through Jesus. So the death of Jesus on the cross was not the end of something, but rather the beginning. It was not a tragedy but a triumph, not a time when Satan won, but a time when he became a public spectacle. The righteous death of one holy man, Jesus Christ the Son of God, released salvation for every person in the world who will acknowledge their sin and embrace the truth of His saving power.

_____, I bless you with full understanding of the gift of complete forgiveness that Jesus Christ offers. I bless you with the desire to surrender control of your life to Jesus as your Lord, allowing Him to be your master, governing you, protecting you, and allowing all other blessings to become a reality for you as you trust Him completely with every part of your life.

I bless you with the joy of regularly seeing Satan's plans to destroy people turned upside down and seeing God bring good out of potentially painful life circumstances. I bless you with the joy of partnering with your Father to take many situations that Satan intends for harm and defeating the enemy's plans for evil and turning bad situations into beauty as you experience your Father's presence with you. I bless you as a normal course of life to see the problems that Satan brings into the world used by God to reveal new wisdom, new grace, new strength, and new freedom, as God makes a public spectacle of His enemy and yours through you. I bless you with God's perspective on the pain and suffering in the world; that it will be an opportunity for you to rise to your calling and live up to a fuller potential than you have known. I bless you with partnering with God for His purposes, using problems as a platform to see Him work in ways that are unmistakably Him. I bless you with these blessings of victory and bringing the victory of the cross forward to the present. I bless you in the name of Jesus of Nazareth, your Lord.

> BE AT PEACE WITH HIM, SO THAT YOU CAN BE COMPLETE, FULFILLED, AND ORDERED IN YOUR INNER LIFE.

Respond with your spirit...

Write your thoughts, etc.

Day 30 Peace With God

_____, listen with your spirit to the Word of God for you. "But he was pierced for our transgressions, he was crushed for our iniquities; the punishment that brought us peace was upon him, and by his wounds we are healed" (Isaiah 53:5). "For he himself is our peace, who has made the two one and has destroyed the barrier, the dividing wall of hostility, by abolishing in his flesh the law with its commandments and regulations. His purpose was to create in himself one new man out of the two, thus making peace, and in this one body to reconcile both of them to God through the cross, by which he put to death their hostility. He came and preached peace to you who were far away and peace to those who were near" (Ephesians 2:14-17).

These two passages sum up the story of mankind in His relationship to God. Peace centers on relationships. In the Old Testament two-thirds of the uses of the word "peace" refer to mankind's having fulfillment, protection, provision, or intimacy because of the presence of God. God yearns to have intimacy with us, to have each one of us be at peace with Him, so that we can be complete, fulfilled, and ordered in our inner lives. Adam and Eve were made without sin, but from the time they sinned, every person has fallen into sin. Sin poses a problem between us and God. Sin is disobedience to God, violation of the standard that God has placed before us. God chose Abraham to be the father of a great nation which we call

> I BLESS YOU WITH PEACE THROUGH HARMONIZING OF YOUR LIFE, BRINGING ALL THE DIFFERENT COMPONENTS OF YOUR LIFE TOGETHER INTO ONE CLEAR PURPOSE, WHICH JESUS CHRIST DESIGNED FOR YOU FROM BEFORE THE FOUNDATION OF THE WORLD.

77

Israel. They had a special relationship with God. He entered into a covenant with them, and He left His presence in that nation for many hundreds of years. Sometimes they were holy and turned to God; sometimes they were sinful and turned away from God, but He remained with them. They remained His chosen people, in contrast to the rest of the nations who were permitted to come to the God of Israel but did not have God residing among them.

Eventually Jesus Christ came to earth, fully God and completely man. He was the only person to live without sin, and He chose to go to death on the cross and pay the price—not for His sins, because He had none, but for our sins. Isaiah said, "He was pierced for our transgressions; he was crushed for our iniquities. The punishment that brought us peace was upon him. And by his wounds we are healed." He died on the cross for the people of Israel who did not know Him fully and for Gentiles who were far from Him and knew less about Him than the Jews. God sent Jesus Christ to do this for those faraway and those who are near, so that we may have peace with Him.

_____, I bless you with the work of the Holy Spirit that gets you past the barrier of sin and into intimacy with your Father and with His Son Jesus. I bless you with peace through harmonizing your life, bringing all the different components of your life together into one clear purpose: the purpose which Jesus Christ designed for you from before the foundation of the world. I bless you with coming into peace with yourself, peace with God, and peace with others through the work of Jesus Christ in removing your sins and repairing your brokenness to bring you to peace. I bless you with knowing that sin erects a barrier that keeps you from knowing all of God that you are supposed to know. Your Father loves you, and He communicates His love to you.

I bless you with understanding the sinfulness of man and the holiness of God. I bless you with a spirit that is profoundly sensitive to right and wrong. I bless you with a high moral standard and a keen desire to experience the peace and pleasure of God. I bless you with desire to be close to God and receive the full work that Christ has already done in His death on the cross. I bless you with understanding in your spirit and your mind the salvation that Jesus Christ offers you, which removes all hostility between you and God and enables you to come into His presence with full peace, reconciled to Him. I bless you with the truth of this wonderful salvation coming to you in a profoundly transforming way, because the Lord Jesus Christ desires it. He desperately wants you to be fully and completely reconciled to Him. I bless you in the name of Jesus of Nazareth, whose crucifixion bought your peace.

Respond with your spirit...

Write your thoughts, etc.

Day 31 God Keeps the Night Watches

_____, I call your spirit to attention. Listen with your spirit to the Word of God for you. "If I say, 'Surely the darkness will hide me and the light become night around me,' even the darkness will not be dark to you; the night will shine like the day, for darkness is as light to you" (Psalm 139:11-12). "There is no dark place, no deep shadow, where evildoers can hide" (Job 34:22). "'Can anyone hide in secret places so that I cannot see him?' declares the Lord. 'Do not I fill heaven and earth?' declares the Lord" (Jeremiah 23:24). Your heavenly Father's faithful, eternal word to you is that darkness is light to Him.

_____, with your spirit take confidence in the Lord your God. Because He is with you, as close as your next breath, and because Jesus lives in you, you have no reason to fear at night. Listen with your spirit to His promises. "He who dwells in the shelter of the Most High will rest in the shadow of the Almighty. I will say of the Lord, 'He is my refuge and my fortress, my God, in whom I trust.' Surely he will save you from the fowler's snare and from the deadly pestilence. He will cover you with his feathers, and under his wings you will find refuge; his faithfulness will be your shield and rampart. You will not fear the terror of night, nor the arrow that flies by day, nor the pestilence that stalks in the darkness, nor the plague that destroys at midday. A thousand may fall at your side, ten thousand at your right hand, but it will not come near you" (Psalm 91:1-7).

Your heavenly Father sustains you with the shield of His presence by night. Receive His confidence deep in your spirit. "But you are a shield around me, O Lord; you bestow glory on me and lift up my head. I lie down and sleep; I wake again, because the Lord sustains me" (Psalm 3:3, 5).

_____, God sings lullabies over you at night. "By day the Lord directs his love, at night his song is with me—a prayer to the God of my life" (Psalm 42:8). Listen with your spirit to His song.

Your spirit can sing in the night watches. "I remembered my songs in the night..." (Psalm 77:6). "On my bed I remember you; I think of you through the watches of the night. Because you are my help, I sing in the shadow of your wings. My soul clings to you; your right hand upholds me" (Psalm 63:6-8). "For the Lord takes delight in His people... Let the saints rejoice in this honor and sing for joy on their beds" (Psalm 149:4-5).

I BLESS YOU WITH ASSURANCE OF HIS HELP AND PRESENCE IN ALL THE MAJESTY OF THE GLORIOUS DETAIL WITH WHICH HE HAS ORDAINED THE LENGTH OF YOUR DAYS.

His praise comforts you with his faithfulness at night. "It is good to praise the Lord and make music to your name, O Most High, to proclaim your love in the morning and your faithfulness at night" (Psalm 92:1-2).

Instead of listening to your fears, listen with your spirit to God counseling you and reassuring you of His promises and His name. "I will praise the Lord, who counsels me; even at night my heart instructs me" (Psalm 16:7). "In the night I remember your name, O Lord ... My eyes stay open through the watches of the night, that I may meditate on your promises" (Psalm 119:55, 148).

Ask God if wakefulness at night is His call to intercession for someone else. "Arise, cry out in the night, as the watches of the night begin; pour out your heart like water in the presence of the Lord..." (Lam. 2:19). Ask God who He wants you to pray for.

God gives sleep, so you can ask Him for it. "...He grants sleep to those he loves" (Psalm 127:2).

When the Lord is your confidence, your sleep is safe and sweet. "I will lie down and sleep in peace, for you alone, O Lord, make me dwell in safety" (Psalm 4:8). "Then you will go on your way in safety, and your foot will not stumble; when you lie down, you will not be afraid; when you lie down, your sleep will be sweet. Have no fear of sudden disaster or of the ruin that overtakes the wicked, for the Lord will be your confidence and will keep your foot from being snared" (Proverbs 3:23-26).

God never sleeps, so you can rest with confidence. "In that day—'Sing about a fruitful vineyard: I, the Lord, watch over it; I water it continually. I guard it day and night so that no one may harm it'" (Isaiah 27:2-3). "My help comes from the Lord, the Maker of heaven and earth. He will not let your foot slip—he who watches over you will not slumber; indeed, he who watches over Israel will neither slumber nor sleep. The Lord watches over you—the Lord is your shade at your right hand; the sun will not harm you by day, nor the moon by night. The Lord will keep you from all harm—He will watch over your life; the Lord will watch over your coming and going both now and forevermore" (Psalm 121:2-8).

I bless you in the name of your eternal God who keeps the night watches.

Respond with your spirit...

Write your thoughts, etc.

Day 32 Strength to Equal Your Days

_____, listen with your spirit to the Word of God for you. "...Your strength will equal your days" (Deuteronomy 33:25). "For to be sure, he was crucified in weakness, yet he lives by God's power. Likewise, we are weak in him, yet by God's power we will live with him to serve you" (2 Corinthians 13:4).

By your Father's strength you have life. I bless you with strength in your spirit for each day. I bless you with waking up every morning knowing that the living God is sustaining, strengthening, and renewing your spirit for the opportunities and problems that He sets before you today. I bless you with knowing that your Father's power provides everything you need today for being who you are called to be and doing acts of obedient service to Him which He appoints for you to do in Jesus' name. I bless you with the assurance of inner quiet, security, and strength, not only for each day, but for the duration of your lifetime. I bless you with assurance of His help and presence in all the majesty of the glorious detail with which He has ordained the length of your days. I bless you with a constant and growing sense of His presence with you for His purposes and His pleasure.

By your Father's promise you have life. _____, listen with your spirit to God's Word. "My comfort in my suffering is this: Your promise preserves my life" (Psalm 119:50). I bless you with your Father renewing your heart and your spirit with His promises. I bless you with recalling the many times that your Father has been with you, has loved you, has taken care of you, has blessed you. I bless you with holding on to promises that He is making to you in the present from His Word and by His Spirit. I bless you with deep understanding that His words are your very life. I bless you with knowing that your faithful Father is watching over His purposes that are not yet completed, promises that await a future time for fulfillment. I bless you with enjoying life, being renewed, refreshed, and restored in your relationship with God and His faithfulness expressed in His Word.

By your Father's life you have life. _____, listen with your spirit to God's Word. "For as the Father has life in himself, so he has granted the Son to have life in himself" (John 5:26). Your Father has life, and He has given His Son the reality of having life in Himself. I bless you with the life that Jesus has that His Father gave Him. I bless you with knowing the life of your Father and of His Son living in your spirit and enlarging your spirit to know Him better and love Him more. I bless you with knowing deep in your spirit that you are alive and well and awake and fully present to life today by the power of His Holy Spirit.

By the power of the Living One you have life. _____, listen with your spirit to God's Word. "Jesus said to her, 'I am the resurrection and the life. He who believes in me will live...'" (John 11:25). I bless you with believing that the Living One lives in you as your life for today. I bless you with appropriating with your spirit the full measure of the life of Jesus within you for today.

By the light of Jesus you have life. _____, listen again with your spirit to God's Word. "In Him was life, and that life was the light of men" (John 1:4). I bless you with light that comes from the life of Jesus living in you and through you. I bless you with His life that lights your way, your relationships, your time, your decisions.

By the words of Jesus you have life. _____, listen again with your spirit to God's Word. "The Spirit gives life; the flesh counts for nothing. The words I have spoken to you are spirit and they are life" (John 6:63). I bless your spirit with hearing and knowing the words that Jesus speaks to you. I bless you with meeting Him daily, spirit to Spirit. I bless you with not doing anything by mere human effort. I bless you with being energized with the life of eternity upon all that you are, think, and do.

I bless you in the name of Jesus of Nazareth, who is your life.

Respond with your spirit...
Write your thoughts, etc.

Day 33 Seeing God's Fingerprints

_____, listen with your spirit to God's Word for you. "Come and see what God has done, how awesome His works in man's behalf!" (Psalm 66:5)

_____, I bless you with seeing your Father's fingerprints on your life. I bless you with your Father's planting reminders of Himself and His majesty everywhere around you. I bless you with considering the heavens and the art of God in nature.

I bless you with appreciating that the heavens declare the glory of God and everything around you proclaims the work of His hands. I bless you with remembering and celebrating His mercy and grace in all that touches you. I bless you with knowing that your Father has made everything beautiful for its own time.

I bless you as He makes himself known to you more and more profoundly and intimately. I bless you with deep awareness that He has planted eternity in your heart and with awe that the whole scope of God's work from beginning to end is so incredible. I bless you with knowing that your Father's plans for your life are too numerous to comprehend or even imagine. I bless you with being able to trace His hand and to understand how particular events fit into His cosmic picture. I bless you with glimpses of His whole design, as His image within you longs to see the beauty of it all, to know the meaning of it all, to discern the ultimate purpose of it all. I bless you with grasping the strategy of heaven, at least in part, but also to entrust those things you don't know to His all-knowing.

I bless you with coming to your heavenly Father, drawing near with your heart and your spirit to Him. I bless you with truly seeing with fresh perspective what your Father has done for you, the awesome miracles He is doing for you. I bless you with seeing with thanksgiving and gratitude God's work in your life and in your world. I bless you with celebrating the heritage of blessings that your Father has invested in you. I bless you with counting your blessings, never ceasing to give glory to God as you were created to do. I bless you with fulfillment in joining the heavenly chorus of worship of your heavenly Father for His character, His availability, His Father-heart, His love, His mercy, and on and on.

I bless you, _____, with unfolding and enlarging your spirit. I bless you with room to breathe free, to become, to grow, to fill the whole frame of God's masterpiece that He is painting of your life. I bless you with receiving your life from the hand of your Father whose plans are marvelous.

I BLESS YOU WITH BEING ABLE TO TRACE HIS HAND AND TO UNDERSTAND HOW PARTICULARS FIT INTO HIS COSMIC PICTURE.

I bless you with appreciation of the awesome, overwhelming creativity and intricacy of your design and the design of everybody and everything in your world. I bless you with more and more revelation into the plans and purposes of your Father's heart for you, in you, and through you, and for others, and for the place and community in which you live. I bless you in the name of Jesus of Nazareth.

Respond with your spirit...

Write your thoughts, etc.

87

Day 34 Faith

_____, listen with your spirit to the Word of
God for you. "My message and my preaching were not with
wise and persuasive words, but with a demonstration of the
Spirit's power, so that your faith might not rest on men's
wisdom, but on God's power." (1 Corinthians 2:4-5)

_____, I bless you with faith that comes by the
power of the Holy Spirit operative in your spirit. I bless you
with faith that is anchored in the Holy Spirit's testimony
to the power of God, not in human reasoning or the
philosophy of man or fickle human emotions.

_____, listen with your spirit to God's Word.
"Yet he [Abraham] did not waver through unbelief regarding
the promise of God, but was strengthened in his faith and
gave glory to God, being fully persuaded that God had
power to do what he had promised." (Romans 4:20-21)

_____, I bless you with the unwavering faith
of Abraham who left his native country and went with God
wherever he led. I bless you with the faith of Abraham that
would wait 25 years for the promise of God. I bless you with
growing stronger and more persuaded by the power of your
faith that brings glory to God. I bless you with being fully
satisfied that God is keeping His word to you, no matter
how long it takes or how contrary your circumstances
might look. I bless you with being fully assured that God is
able and mighty to keep His word. I bless you with being
strengthened in faith by Jesus the author and finisher of
your faith.

_____, listen with your spirit to the Word of
God. "In this you greatly rejoice, though now for a little
while you may have had to suffer grief in all kinds of trials.
These have come so that your faith—of greater worth than

gold, which perishes even though refined by fire—may be proved genuine and may result in praise, glory and honor when Jesus Christ is revealed. Though you have not seen him, you love him; and even though you do not see him now, you believe in him and are filled with an inexpressible and glorious joy." (1 Peter 1:6-8)

_____, I bless you with faith that has been tested and proved genuine. I bless you with seeing the joy on the other side of all kinds of trials. I bless you with faith that is strong and pure like gold. I bless you with knowing how precious your faith is to God, more precious than gold. I bless you with the praise, glory, and honor that it reflects on Jesus for you to trust Him, and I bless you with glory that will be revealed to you when the whole scope of God's plans is made known when Jesus is revealed. I bless you with the faith that loving Him produces and the inexpressible joy that believing Him brings.

THE SUPERNATURAL POWER OF THE HOLY SPIRIT IS WITH YOU TO FILL YOUR HEART WITH ASSURANCE THAT YOUR FATHER LOVES YOU.

_____, listen again with your spirit. "Trust in the Lord with all your heart and lean not on your own understanding; in all your ways acknowledge him, and he will make your paths straight." (Proverbs 3:5-6)

_____, I bless you with confident trust in your Father with all that is in you. I bless you with not depending on your own insight or understanding, because it is skewed and incomplete at best. I bless you with the "yada factor." Yada is the Hebrew word that is translated acknowledge. It means to perceive, understand, distinguish, acquire knowledge, but also to be familiar with, to be aware of in the closest sense, to know at the most intimate level. I bless you with that kind of relationship with your Father. I bless you with knowing your Father intimately and abiding by His will and living in step with His ways in everything. I bless you with knowing His intimate and deep direction of your life. I bless you in the name of Jesus of Nazareth.

Respond with your spirit...

Write your thoughts, etc.

Day 35 Hope

_____, listen with your spirit to the Word of God for you. "…Our Lord Jesus Christ, through whom we have gained access by faith into this grace in which we now stand. And we rejoice in the hope of the glory of God. Not only so, but we also rejoice in our sufferings, because we know that suffering produces perseverance; perseverance, character; and character, hope. And hope does not disappoint us, because God has poured out his love into our hearts by the Holy Spirit, whom he has given us" (Romans 5:1-5).

_____, your Father says Christ Jesus His Son has brought you into the grace of highest privilege, and you can be full of joy now, in problems, troubles, and trials, because you confidently and joyfully look forward to sharing His glory. The Greek word translated hope means desiring some good and confidently expecting to obtain it. The outcome is not in doubt. Your victory is in your Father, in spite of opposition, challenges, or suffering that comes to you. Even when expectation is delayed, when

> I BLESS YOU WITH KNOWING THAT NOTHING IN YOUR PAST, PRESENT, OR FUTURE CAN TAKE HIS LOVE FROM YOU.

the waiting gets long without fulfillment, you can have the confidence of your Father that your adversity is working good for you. Your Father promises that God-given desire leads somewhere—to learning endurance, to developing strength of character, and to confident expectation of seeing the glory of His love for you. This confidence will never disappoint because His love for you will never change. The supernatural power of the Holy Spirit is with you, to fill your heart with assurance that your Father loves you. That's why, as a father, He can tell you gently and firmly, "Be joyful in hope."

_____, listen with your spirit to the Word of God. "But blessed is the man who trusts in the Lord, whose confidence is in Him" (Jeremiah 17:7). "...Then you will know that I am the Lord; those who hope in me will not be disappointed" (Isaiah 49:23).

_____, you are in God's waiting room, anticipating and expecting while you learn the meaning of hope. Hope that is seen is not hope at all. I bless you with hope when your expectation is delayed. One of the Hebrew words for "hope" and "wait" derives from the same root word. The Hebrew words translated "hope" mean confidence, twisting in labor pains, waiting, shelter, expectation, patience, security, trust, enduring, expectancy, something longed for. When your temptation to hopelessness continues without fulfillment, your Father says that those who wait for Him will never be put to shame. Your Father is the God of hope who fills you with all joy and peace as you trust in Him. I bless you with overflowing hope by the power of the Holy Spirit. I bless you with knowing that your Father's eyes are on those who hope, and I bless you with knowing that He rewards those who hope in Him. I bless you with security and safety because your hope is anchored in your Father's love.

_____, listen with your spirit to the Word of God. "Find rest, O my soul, in God alone; my hope comes from him. He alone is my rock and my salvation; He is my fortress, I will not be shaken" (Psalm 62:5-6). "...I know whom I have believed, and am convinced that he is able to guard what I have entrusted to him for that day" (2 Timothy 1:12).

_____, I bless you with rest and quietness in your spirit that come from God. I bless you with a strong sense in your spirit of standing on the solid rock of God's faithfulness and timing. I bless you with unshakable confidence that your Father is in charge of your circumstances. I bless you in your spirit with ascendancy over your soul which may ask the wrong questions. I bless you with asking your Father the right questions as you fix your gaze on Him. I bless you with knowing that there is no valley of trouble that He intends you to pass through without His wisdom and guidance and grace. I bless you with faithfulness and fruitfulness in the face of circumstances that look hopeless.

_____, listen with your spirit to God's Word for you. "God did this so that, by two unchangeable things in which it is impossible for God to lie, we who have fled to take hold of the hope offered to us may be greatly encouraged. We have this hope as an anchor for the soul, firm and secure..." (Hebrews 6:18-19).

_____, I bless you with knowing deeply that your Father cannot and will not lie. I bless you with continued faith and unmovable hope as gifts from God that produce encouragement. I bless you with perfect understanding in your spirit that He will never change His mind about you. I bless your spirit to run to Him as the strong and trustworthy anchor of your soul. I bless you with taking refuge in Him so that you take new courage as you hold on to His character and His promises with confidence. I bless you with remaining in the three-fold cord of faith, hope, and love. I bless you with allowing your Father to replace your burden with His faith, your disappointment with His hope, and your doubts with His love. I bless you with offering Him with your spirit a sacrifice of thanksgiving, with singing songs in the night of your soul, with connecting with your Father in a special and deep way as you praise Him for His unchangeableness. I bless you with unshakable hope, when everything else is shaken. I bless you in the name of Jesus of Nazareth.

Respond with your spirit...

Write your thoughts, etc.

Day 36 Love

_____, listen with your spirit to the Word of God. "For I am convinced that neither death nor life, neither angels nor demons, neither the present nor the future, nor any powers, neither height nor depth, nor anything else in all creation, will be able to separate us from the love of God that is in Christ Jesus our Lord" (Romans 8:38-39).

_____, your Father made you beautiful and beloved. I bless you with receiving the Father-heart of God and His matchless love for you. His love revealed in you is a gold mine of identity and legitimacy from which to live out your birthright confidently and purposefully. I bless you with the belonging, inclusion, and worth that His love nurtures in you. I bless you with being convinced deep in your spirit that nothing in heaven, earth, or hell can separate you from your Father's love. I bless you with knowing that nothing in your past, present, or future can take His love from you. I bless you with being sure of His love in your fears and worries, in your problems and pain, in good times and bad. He promises that because of His love, His power, and His blessing upon you, He causes pain and negative things to be transformed into good, and I bless you with deeply abiding in that truth.

_____, listen with your spirit to God's Word for you. "As the Father has loved me, so have I loved you. Now remain in my love." "I have told you this so that my joy may be in you and that your joy may be complete" (John 15:9,11).

_____, I bless you with being filled with complete and overflowing joy, knowing that Jesus loves you as His Father loves Him. Imagine that! He loves you with the same love that flows between His Father and Him. I bless you with experiencing that rich love of your Father.

I bless you with deep heart identity as God's very own beloved child, securely loved in His family, calling Him "Abba, dear Father." I bless you with seeing in the spirit realm things as they are, the gifts and the presence and hand of your Father, His truth, and His love touches all through your life. I bless you with experiencing your Father's faithful love for you, with your spirit and your heart knowing, feeling, and delighting in the love that your Father expresses to you. I bless you with experiencing that so often that you never doubt your Father's love. I bless you

I BLESS YOU WITH KNOWING DEEP IN YOUR SPIRIT THAT YOUR FATHER'S FAVOR IS UPON YOU; HE LIKES YOU; HE ENJOYS YOU; HE TAKES PLEASURE IN WHO YOU ARE TODAY, REGARDLESS OF WHAT YOU ARE DOING OR HAVE DONE.

with knowing deeply in your spirit the truth that you are accepted, affirmed, and capable. I bless you with receiving God's love that casts out fear. I bless your spirit with being completely persuaded that nothing can separate you from His love.

I bless you with knowing profoundly that God is love. I bless you with being known as a person who is loved by the Lord and who loves the Lord. I bless you with knowing deep in your spirit that your Father's favor is upon you; He likes you; He enjoys you; He takes pleasure in who you are today, regardless of what you are doing or have done. I bless you with profoundly knowing that he finds pleasure in you. I bless you with being secure in your Father's love, having the peace of Jesus in your relationship with your Father. I bless you with receiving the communication of His love to you in a thousand ways. I bless you with creative and unique reminders of your Father's love for you. I bless you with recalling countless times that your Father has been with you, has loved you, has taken care of you, has blessed you. You can do nothing to make Him love you more and nothing to make Him love you less.

I bless and release you to love and be loved, to enjoy life and enjoy your Father and be enjoyed by Him. "And now these three remain: faith, hope, and love. But the greatest of these is love" (I Corinthians 13:13). I bless you with his banner of love over you. I bless you in the name of Jesus of Nazareth.

Respond with your spirit...

Write your thoughts, etc.

Day 37 Spirit, Soul, and Body

_____, listen with your spirit to the Word of God for you. "May God himself, the God of peace, sanctify you through and through. May your whole spirit, soul and body be kept blameless at the coming of our Lord Jesus Christ" (1 Thessalonians 5:23).

I bless you, _____, with a whole spirit, as your Father makes you holy in every way. I bless your spirit with ruling over your soul, not being subordinated to the soul. I bless your spirit as the head and not the tail. I bless you with an enlarged spirit that leads your soul and your body. I bless your spirit with freedom from all captivities. I bless your spirit with the grace and forgiveness to step over any offense and cancel every debt. I bless your spirit with release from bitterness, instead of trying to get repayment. I bless you with freedom from defilement by the poison of bitterness. I bless your spirit with looking to your Father for vindication, as you choose to forgive and release bitterness. I bless you with a healthy dose of repentance for sinful actions. I bless you with looking backward only until your vision is filled with the cross and you meditate on its effective work in your life.

I BLESS YOU WITH GROWING IN INTIMATE KNOWLEDGE OF GOD—HIS PERSON AND CHARACTER—AND THEN, JOINING INTIMACY AND REVELATION LIKE THE DISCIPLES ON THE ROAD TO EMMAUS, WHOSE HEARTS BURNED WITHIN THEM AS JESUS OPENED THE WORDS OF GOD TO THEM.

Listen, _____, with your spirit God's Word for you. "We always thank God for all of you, mentioning you in our prayers. We continually remember before our God and Father your work produced by faith, your labor prompted by love, and your endurance inspired by hope in our Lord Jesus Christ" (1 Thessalonians 1:2-3). Paul speaks of the enduring virtues of faith, love, and hope as the motive for work for the Lord. Amid their faith, hope, and love, the Thessalonian church had the joy of the Lord that transcended their painful circumstances.

_____, I thank God for you. You are a blessing to your Father and to many others. You are a beautiful child in your Father's eyes. I celebrate the good gifts God has given you in His Holy Spirit. I bless you with seeking to live with your spirit saturated with faith, hope, and love. I bless you with the fullness of these essential virtues. I bless you with these three virtues as the basis for your heart motivation and your choices. I bless you with the greatest identity of love that is patient and kind, that does not envy, does not boast, and is not proud. I bless you with love that is not rude, not self-seeking, is not easily angered, and keeps no record of wrongs. I bless you with the virtue of love that does not delight in evil but rejoices with the truth. I bless you with love that always protects, always trusts, always hopes, always perseveres. I bless you with love that never fails (I Corinthians 13:4-8). I bless your spirit with the power to soften hardened hearts with love. Everywhere around you, you see a poor reflection of love. I bless you with anticipation of seeing face to face the One who is love. I bless you with keeping before you faith, hope, and love, and I bless you with the remembrance that the greatest of these is love. I bless you in the name of Jesus of Nazareth.

Respond with your spirit...

Write your thoughts, etc.

Day 38 Colossians 1:9–13

_____, I call your spirit to attention. Listen with your spirit to the Word of God. "For this reason, since the day we heard about you, we have not stopped praying for you and asking God to fill you with the knowledge of his will through all spiritual wisdom and understanding" (Colossians 1:9).

I bless you with spiritual wisdom, with being filled with complete understanding of God's will and His ways in relation to your life. I bless you with asking the right questions and discerning His voice in your spirit and hearing no competing voices. I bless you with spiritual blessings of revelation of the Father, Son, and Holy Spirit.

_____, listen with your spirit to God's Word. "And we pray this in order that you may live a life worthy of the Lord and may please him in every way: bearing fruit in every good work, growing in the knowledge of God" (Colossians 1:10).

I bless you with living a life worthy of the Lord, honoring and pleasing your Father always by the way you live. I bless you with heavenly desires to do good continually, doing kind things for others out of the wellspring of a full and whole spirit. You were created in Christ Jesus for particular purposes, which God prepared in advance for you. Your Savior, the True Vine, says to you, "Remain in me, and I will remain in you. No branch can bear fruit by itself; it must remain in the vine. Neither can you bear fruit unless you remain in me. This is to my Father's glory, that you bear much fruit, showing yourselves to be my disciples. ...I chose you and appointed you to go and bear fruit—fruit that will last..." (John 15:4,8,16).

I bless you with enlarging and increasing your experience of the magnificence of your Father. I bless you with growing in intimate knowledge of God—His person and character—and then, joining intimacy and revelation like the disciples on the road to Emmaus, whose hearts burned within them as Jesus opened the words of God to them.

_____, listen with your spirit to God's Word. "...Being strengthened with all power according to his glorious might so that you may have great endurance and patience..." (Colossians 1:11).

I bless you with being strengthened with His glorious power, so that you will have all the patience and endurance you need, with joy. I bless you with three-fold staying power in time of distress—strength, power, might from Him, by His glory and for His glory. I bless you with withstanding all your fears in the Spirit of power and love and a sound mind (2 Timothy 1:7). I bless you with knowing your God deeply so that you will be strong and do great exploits. I bless you with being a living demonstration of new manifestations of God's ability and wisdom and power.

I bless you with inexpressible joy imparted by the Holy Spirit, not depending on circumstances. I bless you with positively investing in this season of preparation, enduring with joy, not knowing what God is up to. I bless you with aggressively paying the price to do the daily spiritual exercises required. I bless you with not rationalizing away or backing out of the call of God on your life. I bless you with great forward-looking vision to withstand present pressure of birthing pains for the joy set before you.

_____, listen with your spirit to the Word of God to you. "... Giving thanks to the Father, who has qualified you to share in the inheritance of the saints in the kingdom of light. For he has rescued us from the dominion of darkness and brought us into the kingdom of the Son he loves..." (Colossians 1:12-13).

I bless you with an overflow of deep gratitude in your spirit, as you thank your Father for allowing you to inherit all covenant blessings that belong to God's holy people, who live in His kingdom of light. I bless you with knowing the hope of His calling and what a rich and glorious inheritance He has in His saints. I bless you with sharing with a family of faith that lives in the light with clear and vulnerable relationships. I bless your spirit with a flood of light so you can understand the wonderful future He has promised you.

I bless you with knowing your dominion over all the power of darkness. I bless you with the eyes of your heart being enlightened to know your Father's incredibly great power for you, the same working of His mighty strength that raised Christ from the dead and seated Him at His right hand in the heavenly realms. I bless you with knowing with certainty that He is far above all rule and authority, power and dominion, and every title that can be given in this present age. _____, you are blessed that God has put all things under the authority of Christ and appointed Him to be head over everything for the church, which is His body (Colossians 1:18). You are blessed in the name of Jesus of Nazareth, who fills everything everywhere with His presence.

Respond with your spirit...

Write your thoughts, etc.

Day 39 Sound of Heaven

_____, listen with your spirit to God's Word.
"The Lord came and stood there, calling as at the other
times, 'Samuel! Samuel!' Then Samuel said, 'Speak, for
your servant is listening'" (1 Samuel 3:10).

I bless you with awakening your spirit to the voice
of God and tuning your spiritual ears to Him. Your creator
God spoke and out of the void, all things had their being
and order. In tuning your ears to hear, I bless you with
becoming like the child, Samuel, in your response to God's
calling. I bless you with being fully engaged with listening
as a process, a training which you practice, and a deliberate
choice you make. Spirit, definitely and definitively be in
control and in dominion over your soul, mind, and body.
Cleanse, awaken, and alert your personal sound portal
(your ears) so that what you hear will not be dull or defiled. I
bless you with awakened, deeply cleansed, alert, and finely-
tuned ears to hear, so that the sound of heaven will open
the spirit realm to you in God's time.

I bless you with quieting your soul in order to hear
more clearly with your spiritual ears. Your listening is very
active, not passive. God speaks to you in many creative
ways, and I bless you with setting your spiritual ears to
His frequency to hear His voice profoundly in all of its
manifestations. I bless you with hearing the Father of your
spirit in His Word, by faith (faith comes by hearing and
hearing by the Word of God), through dreams and visions,
through others, by His Holy Spirit, through His creation, etc.
The heavens declare the glory of the Lord (Psalm 19:1), and
I bless you with hearing their declaration.

Your salvation depended on His voice calling you,
and your response to Him was music to His ears. I bless
you with the posture and willingness of spirit, that makes
you able and ready to hear every word from God. I bless

you with listening on the inside with commitment to obey. I bless you with sensitive ears and focused spiritual attention on listening to God, that when He speaks, your receiver is tuned to His frequency. I bless you with a hearing spirit and an understanding heart to discern between good and evil (1 Kings 3:9). I bless you with clearing out the static and interference so that you have a clear channel.

Enlightened spiritual hearing is vital to your spirit life, salvation, service, spiritual warfare, and your worship. From the very beginning Israel was called to listen. "Hear, O Israel, the Lord your God is One" (Deuteronomy 6:4). This word "shema" ("hear") means to listen and obey. God has called every generation to hear Him and act on what He says, from the children of Israel gathered to receive the Ten Commandments, to the voice of the prophets crying in the wilderness, "Prepare the way of the Lord," to the words of our Lord Jesus in Revelation, "He who has ears, let him hear." God will honor your spirit's willingness to hear with the view to obey no matter what. Hear the prophet's voice crying to make way for a new visitation of God among His people, and respond positively to the Holy Spirit.

> I BLESS YOU WITH HEARING THE SOUND OF THE TRUMPET THAT CALLS YOU TO READINESS FOR BATTLE, THE SOUND JUST OVER THE TREETOPS THAT SIGNALS THE TIMING FOR BATTLE, AND THE SHOUTS OF VICTORY IN THE CAMP.

I bless you with a warrior's keen hearing in your spirit. In times of spiritual battle, it is crucial to tune your ears to hear your commander. I bless you with hearing the sound of the trumpet that calls you to readiness for battle, the sound just over the treetops that signals the timing for battle, and the shouts of victory in the camp.

I bless you with a worshiping spirit. "Holy, holy, holy is the Lord our God, the Lord God Almighty, who was and is and is to come" (Revelation 4:8). "Worthy is the Lamb to receive all praise and glory and wisdom and thanksgiving and honor and power and strength" (Revelation 5:11). I bless you with worship that is an echo of the proclamation of all of heaven. I bless you with singing in your spirit and resonating in your spirit in the same key as the sound of heaven, keeping time with the beat of heavenly rhythm. There are new songs to hear and sing to the Lord: songs of deliverance; songs of victory; sweet love songs from your Bridegroom; songs of comfort; songs of joy; songs of praise; songs you sing; songs you join in singing; and songs the Lord sings over you. I bless you with open heavens to hear and respond to the sound of heaven.

I bless you with knowing the voice of your Shepherd. Jesus said that his sheep know His voice and follow Him (John 10:27). I bless you with active and accurate listening for deliverance, for freedom, for victory, for direction, for comfort. I bless you with hearing in your spirit all that is vital to possessing your birthright and understanding your legitimacy, for affirmation, for time, timing, and seasons. I bless you with a holy, clean sound portal that is vital to your life as a child of your Father, for it leads you into deeper and sweeter intimacy with Him and more responsiveness to Him. I bless you with satisfaction of your longing to hear Him say, "This is my child in whom I am well pleased" (Matthew 3:17), and, "Well done, good and faithful servant, enter my rest" (Matthew 25:21). I bless you in the name of the Father of your spirit.

Respond with your spirit...

Write your thoughts, etc.

Day 40 Time: A Season for Everything

_____, listen with your spirit to the Word of God for you. "There is a time for everything, and a season for every activity under heaven: a time to be born and a time to die, a time to plant and a time to uproot, a time to kill and a time to heal, a time to tear down and a time to build, a time to weep and a time to laugh, a time to mourn and a time to dance, a time to scatter stones and a time to gather them, a time to embrace and a time to refrain, a time to search and a time to give up, a time to keep and a time to throw away, a time to tear and a time to mend, a time to be silent and a time to speak, a time to love and a time to hate, a time for war and a time for peace" (Ecclesiastes 3:1-8).

_____, I bless you with knowing that your Father has appointed time as the stage for His eternal purposes. With these fourteen pairs of opposites, I bless you with knowing that your Father has appointed and now oversees your position in history, the times and seasons, the events and the experiences, the character and significance of all things that pertain to you. I bless you with knowing His direction of your life, when He doesn't let you see the end from the beginning, so that you will seek Him and His heart and His wisdom at all times. All of time serves His overarching plan, even when life seems senseless and without aim or explanation. I bless you with knowing that everything in your life unfolds under the eye of His providence, even when the pieces don't seem to fit and God's ways are a mystery to you. I bless you with knowing the certainty of how you fit into His time and space, history and the future. In Esther 4:14, it is said of Queen Esther, "Who knows but that you have come to royal position for such a time as this?"

I bless you, _____, with knowing that your Father's appointed and anointed time for everything is beautiful from His perspective of eternity. I bless you with trusting His bigger composite picture, when you can only see the particulars. I bless you with being in step and on time, not running ahead or lagging behind. I bless you with sensitivity to the seasons of the Spirit, the movement of the Spirit, and the moment of the Spirit.

I bless your spirit with an anointing for time and timeliness. When it is time to give birth or to die, I bless you with knowing your Father's birthing seasons and letting die those works of the flesh that are not His. I bless you with knowing your Father's timing to plant a new vision or dream and to pluck up something that is past its season and is already dead. I bless you with your Father's time to heal the soul and kill the lies it has believed. I bless you with your Father's time to build or to tear down, and I pray that you will not erect idols or monuments to works that He is not presently blessing. I bless you with your Father's time to laugh about what makes Him laugh and to weep about what makes Him weep. I bless you with your Father's time to dance, that you will dance with abandon with the Lover of your soul. I bless you with your Father's time to mourn those things that break His heart. I bless you with your Father's time to scatter seed and time to rejoice gathering in the harvest.

I bless you with your Father's time to embrace those people, values, and purposes that He blesses and to refrain from affirming anything that is not His vision for you. I bless you with your Father's time to search for the hidden treasures of love and wisdom, for hope and faith, and to give up as worthless all self-effort and striving. I bless you with your Father's time to keep that which is silver, gold, and precious stones and to throw away all that is wood, hay, and stubble. I bless you with your Father's time to mend relationships and to tear away from soul ties which He did not author. I bless you with your Father's time to be silent, and know when it's time to speak. I bless you with knowing the time of your Father's dealing in another person's life, and whether you are to be involved, and how. I bless you with your Father's time to love what He loves and to hate what He hates with righteous passion. I bless you with your Father's time for war with the real enemy and His time for peace because of the grace of the cross.

_____, your times are safely in His hands. I bless you with enjoying your Father's good gift of time, and I bless you with being squarely 100% present to the current moment to savor all its richness. I bless you with humbly submitting to, believing in, and trusting Him for the outcome. I bless you and entrust you to God and the word of His grace—the message of His heart that is able to build you up and give you an inheritance with all those He has set apart for Himself. I bless you in the name of Jesus of Nazareth.

Respond with your spirit...

Write your thoughts, etc.

Day 1 Jehovah-Jireh

_____, listen with your spirit to the Word of God. "Abraham looked up and there in a thicket he saw a ram caught by its horns. He went over and took the ram and sacrificed it as a burnt offering instead of his son. So Abraham called that place The Lord Will Provide. And to this day it is said, 'On the mountain of the Lord it will be provided'" (Genesis 22:13-14).

The name Jehovah-Jireh has been incorrectly applied to refer to God providing for material needs. The context of this passage shows that God's provision is a sacrifice to cover the sin of mankind. The ram was God's foreshadowing of the redemption provided through His Son centuries later on that same mountain. Christ the worthy Lamb of God died to fulfill the name Jehovah-Jireh.

_____, I bless you with deep consciousness of sin and knowing that God has provided an acceptable sacrifice. I bless you with understanding that your Father wants excellence from you, but not as a way for you to earn a position of favor or acceptability with Him. That price has already been paid. There is nothing left for you to earn in His heart. You can do nothing to make Him love you more, and you can do nothing to make Him love you less. Jesus already proved that at the cross. Your best would never be good enough to prove your love for God. I bless you with knowing profoundly that God is love, and also, with experiencing deep gratitude for the price He paid with the life of His Son for you to be His. At the same time, I bless you with being willing at all times to give Him everything you are and all you have as an act of love and submission.

I bless you, _____, with deep brokenness over your own sinfulness and deep willingness to run to the arms of your forgiving Father who has declared you unconditionally loved and accepted. I bless you with knowing that there is a Redeemer provided by Jehovah-Jireh, and His name is Jesus. I bless you with wonder, awe, and worship rising up in your spirit at knowing that you are so profoundly loved for all time.

_____, I bless you with deep brokenness over the sinfulness of others in your world, but not with condemnation or judgment. I bless you with directing your heart and your spirit to others who have done wrong, to hold out the redeeming hope of God's forgiveness, cleansing, and healing through your healed heart and His grace. I bless you in the name of Jehovah-Jireh, Amen.

Respond with your spirit...

Write your thoughts, etc.

Day 2 Jehovah-Rophe

_____, I call your spirit to attention in the name of Jehovah-Rophe. I bless you with understanding the boundaries of God. Jehovah-Rophe is the name that the Lord gave in revealing Himself after Israel had come out of Egypt. In Egypt they had been cared for by Egyptian doctors because they had Egyptian diseases. When they entered the desert, God healed everyone. There was not a sick person in all of Israel, and God had left the Egyptian diseases and the Egyptian doctors behind. But they ran into a problem with poison water. After God healed the water, He told them that He would spare them from the diseases of the Egyptians, IF they would obey His principles and follow His commands. They didn't even know at that time what the commands were. They had yet to arrive at Mt. Sinai. God had not given the law, but He promised them that the laws He gave would keep them healthy. He invited them to stay healthy by staying inside the perimeters of those laws.

_____, God has called you to be highly creative, to color outside the lines of your secular and religious culture. Your gifting, your specific anointing is to see new principles in God's word, to understand new facets of the nature of God, and to find new applications of the nature of God in the contemporary culture. I bless that in you. I release you from the limitations of a culture that will bind you to something smaller than that which God has called you to. We celebrate your creativity and your ability to color outside the lines of your culture.

_____, I bless you with a profound and holy reverence for the boundaries that God establishes through His law. While you are thinking outside the box, while you are creating paradigms that others have not thought of, you must stay within the paradigm. Stay within the pattern, within the rules and the laws that God has established in His Word for you. I bless you with being a free spirit regarding the traditions of men, but I bless you with a profound fear of the Lord that causes you to respect the perimeters that God has established to keep you safe and whole.

_____, I bless you with being mighty in spirit. I bless you with avoiding the influences that will cripple you and make you small. I bless you with avoiding the diseases of the spirit and soul and body that will keep you from fulfilling your birthright. I bless you with a progressive revelation of the will of God, the principles of God, the mandates of God. I bless you with a willing heart to stay within those boundaries while you relentlessly violate the boundaries of the culture around you in order to bring God to them in a new way. I bless you, beloved child, in the name of Jehovah-Rophe. I bless you with celebrating the boundaries and possessing your birthright as you remain whole, holy, and wholly within those boundaries. I bless you in the name of the Father and of the Son and of the Holy Spirit, Amen.

Respond with your spirit...
Write your thoughts, etc.

Day 3 Jehovah-Rophe

_____, I call your spirit to attention in the name of Jesus of Nazareth. Listen to the Word of God for you. "He said, 'If you listen carefully to the voice of the Lord your God and do what is right in his eyes, if you pay attention to his commands and keep all his decrees, I will not bring on you any of the diseases I brought on the Egyptians, for I am the Lord, who heals you'" (Exodus 15:26).

The context of the name Jehovah-Rophe is not about healing the sick but staying healthy by following the principles that God gave Israel. This is preventive health through getting clean and staying clean.

_____, you are the product of generational blessings and curses which you inherited from your parents. You were born with both a gold mine and a toxic waste dump. Ideally, your parents would have cleaned up their physical toxicity, emotional woundedness, and spiritual baggage before having children, but they did not know to do so. Even if they had done so, the job is never perfectly done. They unfortunately passed on some negatives to you. The good news is that your Father is not limited by the imperfections of your parents.

Since it is your heavenly Father's desire that you be made whole in spirit, soul, and body, I bless you, _____ with the blessing of the covenant name of Jehovah-Rophe, your healer. I bless you with cleansing in your spirit from defilement of past generations and from your own wrong choices. I bless you with God's sanctifying your spirit to such a degree that you hunger and thirst for the will and Word of God and the communion of His Holy Spirit.

Your Father is the healer of broken hearts, so I bless you with healing from broken-heartedness. I bless

you with a spirit that is healthy, alive, and alert through His
healing presence. I bless you with cleansing in your soul
from every generational soul wound and stronghold of lies.
I bless you with the cleansing blood of Jesus for negative
words spoken to you, about you, or against you. I bless
you with a washing away of all defilements of mind, will,
and emotion. I release you to love and be loved, to enjoy
life and enjoy your Father and be enjoyed by Him, to have
peace with yourself, with others, and with God. I bless you
with freedom to hear from God, to respond to Him, and to
be used by Him as a restorer, healer, and counselor in your
lifetime.

I bless you, _____, with cleansing of your
physical body from susceptibility to diseases in the world.
I bless you with your Father's cleansing of your blood,
since the life is in the blood. I bless you with health and
wholeness in your autoimmune system, which is anchored
by the blood stream. I bless you with health in every organ
and system and cell of your body. I bless you in the name of
Jehovah-Rophe, Amen.

Respond with your spirit...

Write your thoughts, etc.

Day 4 Jehovah-Nissi

_____, I call your spirit to attention in the name of Jehovah-Nissi, God who promised to be at war against the Amalekites from generation to generation. The context of the story is of Moses having to lead his people into battle when they weren't ready to go to war. They were attacked by the Amalekites. As he lifted his hands to the Lord, the Lord warred on behalf of Israel.

_____, I bless your spirit with knowing when to war and when to lift your hands to the Lord. There will be seasons when God calls you to use the greatest of your strength. There will be seasons when God presses you to the wall and yet expects you to work hard, like Israel had to make bricks; then they had to make bricks in a harder way without straw. Then they had to march during the middle of the night to escape from Egypt. There will be times when God will celebrate the gifts that He has placed in you, when He will celebrate your strength. At times God will place you in a context where every talent and ability that you possess can be brought to the front and be used to make changes in the kingdom. That is good. That is fine. That is excellent. That is the will of God.

But there will be times, _____, when God will very specifically put you in a place where everything that you have is not good enough, where you have to do something you have never done before. Enemies that you have never irritated will seek to attack you just because they are opportunistic. I bless you, _____, with having the courage not to depend on a skillset that is inadequate but to have the courage to lift your hands up to God on the mountaintop and ask Jehovah-Nissi to war for you. Because where you are inexperienced against any enemy, Jehovah-Nissi has the experience of the ages. Where you don't know how to do it, Jehovah-Nissi has done it endless times.

Where you have not walked that way before, Jehovah-Nissi has worn a path with the mighty tread of His feet.

_____, Jehovah-Nissi has promised and recorded in Scripture that He cannot lie, that He will be at war against the opportunistic coyote, the spirit of Amalek that prowls around. It never attacks directly but takes advantage of your vulnerabilities, takes advantage of the opportune times of transition when you are not ready for war. Jehovah-Nissi has promised to war on your behalf.

_____, I bless you with finding profound security in Jehovah-Nissi, celebrating your giftedness while always knowing that Jehovah-Nissi is there for those battles that He permits which you don't anticipate. He anticipates the battles that blindside you on a path that you've never walked before. Israel did not know the desert area. The Amalekites lived there. Israel didn't know the safe places, the high places, the hidden places. They didn't know how to craft an effective war strategy. They just went out and bumbled around while Moses stood on the mountain with his hands lifted high.

_____, celebrate your areas of strength, but when you are in a new area and the enemy attacks you and you don't know what to do or how to do or where to do it, go to the mountaintop. Lift your hands and let Jehovah-Nissi war on your behalf. I bless you with knowing Jehovah-Nissi experientially in your generation. I bless you in the name of the Father and of the Son and of the Holy Spirit, Amen.

Respond with your spirit...

Write your thoughts, etc.

Day 5 Jehovah-Nissi

_____, listen with your spirit to the Word of God. "Moses built an altar and called it The Lord is My Banner. He said, 'For hands were lifted up to the throne of the Lord. The Lord will be at war against the Amalekites from generation to generation'" (Exodus 17:15-16).

Jehovah-Nissi, the Lord my Banner, is a covenant name of your Father God. The Amalekites were predators and bullies who preyed on the young, the old, the weak, the stragglers around the edges of the company of the Israelites. They attacked the Israelites as they were coming out of Egypt. God does not appreciate physical or spiritual bullies. Moses went up on a hill with the staff of the Lord in his hands. As long as he held the staff up, Joshua was winning the battle in the valley below. This verse promises that God will be at war with Amalek forever.

_____, you have a strong and available heavenly Father who does not tolerate the spiritual bullies that try to prey on you. I bless you with His protection against being victimized and exploited personally by spiritual strongmen. I bless you with freedom in your spirit from the presence of unusual or persistent opposition and harassment. I bless you with the victory of the Lord as you lift up your hands to the throne of God. I bless you with believing your Father's word that He has an endless hatred of

I BLESS YOU WITH BREATHING FREELY IN YOUR SPIRIT ON A NEW AND DEEPER LEVEL. I BLESS YOU WITH A YIELDED MIND THAT WALKS MORE AND MORE IN STEP WITH JESUS.

the predator spirit that would assail you. I bless you with freedom from emotional bondage and captivity in your spirit. I bless you with breathing freely in your spirit on a new and deeper level. I bless you with a yielded mind that walks more and more in step with Jesus. I bless you with being ransomed from the empty lives of your forefathers. I bless you with throwing off generational curses from your bloodline and putting the cross of Jesus Christ between you and them to be set free. I bless you with a fresh start, a clean break, and freedom from the power of generational predatory assignments.

I bless you with being set free to worship on a new level as Jehovah Nissi clears the air of your enemies in testimony of His glory. I bless you with abiding under the shadow of the Almighty and taking refuge in the Most High God, your Father. I bless you with those who make deposits in you that enrich your spirit.

I bless you with your Father's protection from financial predators who would enrich themselves at your expense. I bless you with protection from opportunists. I bless you with those who invest in you, instead of draining you. I bless you with financial favor in the marketplace, and with people who seek to benefit you and help you.

I bless you with the Lord your Banner encamping around you to protect you physically at all times. I bless you with drawing near to God and trusting him in times of trouble, and not straggling out on the edges of disobedience. May the victory of His redemption be yours at all times. I bless you with instant obedience with a willing spirit, so that the shield of God's favor is always around you.

Listen again, _____, with your spirit to God's Word. "So shall they fear the name of the Lord from the west, and His glory from the rising of the sun; when the enemy comes in like a flood, the Spirit of the Lord will lift up a standard against him" (Isaiah 59:19 NKJV). What a splendid picture your Father paints! When the enemy floods in, affecting every area of your life all at once, the Lord will lift His banner against him. We hold high this standard and ask the wind of the Spirit to cause it to fly so all can see the name written upon it. He who has delivered will still deliver. Hold the banner high in your spirit, your thoughts, and your actions.

I bless you, _____, with knowing His banner of love over you. I bless you with faith and peace, knowing that your Father is trustworthy. I bless you with knowing whom you have believed and being persuaded that He is able to keep that which you have committed to Him. I bless you with ministering spirits to bring what you need, to bring you to your Father's safe place. I bless you with becoming a safe place for others, a shelter, and a refuge with power to heal by the blessing of your presence. I bless you in the name of Jesus, your Jehovah-Nissi, who gave His all for you because He loves you.

Respond with your spirit...

Write your thoughts, etc.

Day 6 Jehovah-Shalom

_____, I call your spirit to attention in the name of Jehovah-Shalom. I bless you with peace that comes from being in the center of the will of the covenant-keeping God. I bless you with knowing in your life and in your spirit the presence of God amid chaos. I bless you with knowing in your spirit that God is pleased with you even when the plans of man go awry.

I bless you with knowing the peace that comes from Jehovah-Shalom in the middle of the turmoil of a community and a culture that has rejected the God whom you serve. I bless you with having peace when you have to stand alone against an entire culture. I bless you with having the peace of God in a supernatural fashion, as when God's peace filled up Gideon's soul, but then drained out again. As the circumstances of life drew him down quickly, he was up and then down. I bless you with not being up and down but being refilled and refilled and filled again, by one experience after another of the greatness of the peace of God as you move through turmoil to peace.

God has called you, _____, to be a changer of cultures. He has caused you to be at a place of transformation in battle. When men and spiritual enemies oppose you, I bless you with deep experiential knowledge of Jehovah-Shalom. I bless you with having peace that is not only sufficient for you, but is sufficient for those that will look at you and follow after you. I bless you with knowledge of God so great that it overflows, and you walk with the anointing of His presence, so that peace flows from you to those around you who do not yet know your God. I bless your spirit with being large enough to embrace the will of God and the presence of God.

I bless you with not only knowing the history of God's intervention but with experiencing an accumulated

history of God's personal intervention in your own life.
I bless you, beloved child, with knowing Jehovah-Shalom
who will enable you to stand your ground and wait and do
nothing when it is time to wait for the fullness of His timing.
I bless you with ears to hear so that you will have absolute
confidence when it is time to move and when it is time to
wait, when it is time to accumulate people around you
and when it is time to release those who have gathered
around you.

I bless you with going into battle without a sword.
I bless you with being so confident of God's strategy
and having so much peace that you—like Gideon, who
went into battle with a trumpet and a light instead of a
sword—will take the unconventional tools of the knowledge
and the ways of God into a battle where others would take
armament. I bless you with having such harmony between
your life and the ways of God that you can walk in the
peace of God. I bless you with having the same certainty
that Gideon had to say, "Jehovah-Shalom." I bless you with
the blessings of Jehovah-Shalom in the name of the Father
and of the Son and of the Holy Spirit, Amen.

Respond with your spirit...

Write your thoughts, etc.

Day 7 Jehovah-Shalom

_____, I call your spirit to attention in the name
of Jehovah-Shalom. Listen to the Word of God for you.
"When the angel of the Lord appeared to Gideon, he said,
'The Lord is with you, mighty warrior.' 'But sir,' Gideon
replied, 'if the Lord is with us, why has all this happened
to us? Where are all His wonders that our fathers told us
about…? But now the Lord has abandoned us and put us
into the hand of Midian.' The Lord turned to him and said,
'Go in the strength you have and save Israel out of Midian's
hand. Am I not sending you?… I will be with you, and you
will strike down all the Midianites together.' The Lord said to
him, 'Peace! Do not be afraid.' And Gideon built an altar to
the Lord there and named it The Lord is Peace…" (Judges
6:12-14,16,23-24).

Jehovah-Shalom is a compound covenant name
of your Father. God addressed Gideon, threshing wheat
in a winepress, while he was hiding from his enemy the
Midianites, who were marauders. They would swoop down
at harvest time and take what the Israelites had worked
hard to cultivate and grow. Gideon knew that God had
done miracles for his forefathers, but he could not see the
presence of God in his present circumstance. Therefore, he
had no peace. At the end of the day, nothing had changed
and the Midianites were still in the land, but Gideon knew
that God was with him, and that made all the difference.

_____, I bless you with the birthright of peace
in all circumstances. I bless you with your Father's peace
saturating you even in the most distressing circumstances.
I bless you with experiencing clearly the peaceful presence
of the Holy Spirit when in trouble. I bless you with feeling
the peace of the presence of your Father with you. I bless
you with understanding that problems in your life are not
evidence that your Father is not present with you. I bless

you with knowing that he has not abandoned you to your enemies. I bless you with peace and calmness of spirit and soul in spite of terrible inconvenience or devouring loss, because you know that your Father is very near. His nearness is sweet, and wonderful, and good. I bless you with honoring him when you can't see him with your physical eyes at work in your world. I bless you with not doubting in the dark what God has told you in the light. I bless you with your Father comforting you when you mourn and giving you the oil of gladness and garments of praise, so that you can say, "He gives and takes away; my heart will choose to say, 'Blessed be the name of the Lord.'"

I bless you, _____, with the perspective of your Father who knows the end from the beginning. I bless you with not magnifying the presence of enemies or trials or problems to seem bigger than the Sovereign Lord of the universe. I bless you with gazing at your Father and glancing at your problems. I bless you with knowing that your Father is available to help you at all times with all that you need. I bless you with a river of peace flowing over you and permeating everything you are and everything you do. I bless you with a river of peace that flows out from your spirit and washes over those around you. I bless you with the smile of your Father whispering to your heart and spirit, "Your peace based in your trust in me pleases me very much." I bless you in the name of Jesus, your Jehovah-Shalom, Amen.

Respond with your spirit...
Write your thoughts, etc.

Day 8 Jehovah-Rohe

_____, listen with your spirit to the Word of God. "The Lord is my shepherd, I shall not be in want. He makes me lie down in green pastures, he leads me beside quiet waters, he restores my soul. He guides me in paths of righteousness for his name's sake. Even though I walk through the valley of the shadow of death, I will fear no evil, for you are with me; your rod and your staff, they comfort me. You prepare a table before me in the presence of my enemies. You anoint my head with oil; my cup overflows. Surely goodness and love will follow me all the days of my life, and I will dwell in the house of the Lord forever" (Psalm 23:1-6).

Jehovah Rohe, the Lord your Shepherd, is a compound covenant name of God. Psalm 23 presents the gift of security given to the sheep by the shepherd. Sheep do not lie down unless they feel secure. The environment must communicate safety to them. Sheep require a green pasture providing an abundance of food and still waters from which to drink, because sheep do not drink from rushing waters.

_____, I bless you with a sense of safety and security in your world provided by the protecting presence, power, wisdom, and love of your Father. Lambs are born knowing their mother's voice, and they quickly learn the shepherd's voice, so I bless you with knowing the reassuring voice of your Shepherd. I bless you with the settled assurance that you have everything you need from the hand of your Shepherd. I bless you with the contentment of knowing that you lack nothing that is good for you.

I bless you with resting in green meadows and experiencing His leading you beside peaceful streams. I rejoice with you that your spirit has a peaceful place in Him to be at home and at rest. I bless you with knowing that He is renewing your strength and your spirit day by day. I rejoice with you that He daily bears your burdens and infuses you with His strength, through which you can do all things in Him.

I bless you with His guidance along right paths, bringing honor to His name. I bless you to not have to walk through life alone because the Holy Spirit guides you in the way you should go and leads you into the way of truth. I rejoice with you that He stakes His own reputation on leading you in righteous paths.

Even when sheep must pass through a dangerous valley on their way from mountain pastures to the lowlands, the presence of the shepherd provides security in the time and place of potential danger. I bless you with being unafraid, because your Shepherd is close beside you, even when you walk through the shadows of dark valleys. I praise God with you for the order of the universe, which He holds together, so that nothing takes Him by surprise. I bless you with habitual confidence in that. I rejoice with you that as death had no power over Jesus, death has no power over you. I bless you with freedom from fear.

I bless you with knowing the protecting rod and comforting staff of your Shepherd. I rejoice with you that Jesus went through the pain and difficulties of human life so He could fully understand and identify with your needs. I bless you with comforting others with the comfort with which He comforts you.

I bless you with a feast of your Father's presence in the presence of your enemies. I rejoice with you that He is your Mighty Warrior. I rejoice with you for the power you have when you speak the name of Jesus. Your Father honors that name above all others, so speak it quickly when you are in trouble or danger.

I bless you with anointing oil for your head, for healing and soothing and blessing. I bless you with knowing that you are welcome, wanted, needed, and honored in your world. I rejoice with you that the dreams and treasures of your heart are safe with Him.

I bless you with a cup that overflows with blessings from the hand of your Father. I rejoice with you over the good gifts He has given you, to His delight and yours. I bless you with all the treasures of His house. I bless you with being at home there.

I bless you with experiencing His goodness and unfailing love which pursues you all the days of your life. I bless you with being acutely aware of the benefits and the responsibilities of the love He has for you.

I bless you with knowing you have a secure place at the table in your Father's house forever. I bless you with knowing the belonging, connectedness, safety, and security of His house. I bless you with knowing that Jesus, your hope of glory, lives in you. I rejoice with you in thanksgiving that He has awakened your spirit to know Him profoundly in these ways. I bless you in the name of Jesus, your Shepherd, Jehovah-Rohe.

Respond with your spirit...

Write your thoughts, etc.

Day 9 Jehovah-Tsidkenu

_____, I call your spirit to attention in the name of Jehovah-Tsidkenu, the Lord your Righteousness. The story behind this name arose from a prophecy to Israel during a time when their spiritual and political leaders were not doing the work of God. They were abusing the people. The people were suffering not from neglect but from raw abuse by their leaders. Listen with your spirit as I read the Word of God to you. God spoke this word: "'The days are coming,' declares the Lord, 'when I will raise up to David a righteous Branch, a King who will reign wisely and do what is just and right in the land. In his days Judah will be saved, and Israel will live in safety, and this is the name by which he will be called, the Lord our Righteousness'" (Jeremiah 23:5-6).

_____, while the blessing and the name apply specifically to Jesus Christ, Son of David, we are to walk in the fullness of who Jesus is. God has called us into those areas of leadership to demonstrate the righteousness of God by weaving principles together in a life-giving way to nurture the sheep. These sheep have been either abandoned or traumatized by leaders who do not know God or who are not conformed to His character.

I bless you, child of the Most High God, with knowing the principles of God's Word. I bless you with an anointing for seeing how to multiply one principle upon another for an exponential effect. I bless you to be a life-giving elder for your community in the moment that God calls you to do so. I bless you with an anointing for leadership. I bless you with not only knowing the Word but knowing how to use the Word as an elder, in order to bring life to the community which God has called you to heal.

I bless you with being a skilled workman who has learned from those who have gone before and understands

127

the principles of wise, godly leadership. In the name of the Lord your Righteousness, I bless you with going beyond the things that others have done. I bless you with raising the standard in your eldership. The day that God calls you to be a mighty man or woman in a community by speaking the life of God into that community, I bless you with knowing new and different ways to weave God's principles together.

I bless each day of your life with having value and not being wasted. I bless you with the people and circumstances that God brings into your life and the diversity of your ministry experiences contributing to the goal of your being an incarnation of the Lord our Righteousness. I bless you with not just the absence of sin, but the skill and the wisdom of weaving together the principles of leadership to be life-giving and to heal the community, so as to bring the community members collectively into possessing their birthright. I bless you with being an incarnation of the Lord our Righteousness. I bless you in the name of the Father and of the Son and of the Holy Spirit, Amen.

Respond with your spirit...
Write your thoughts, etc.

Day 10 Jehovah-Tsidkenu

_____, listen with your spirit to the Word of God to you. "'The days are coming,' declares the Lord, 'when I will raise up to David a righteous Branch, a King who will reign wisely and do what is just and right in the land. In his days Judah will be saved, and Israel will live in safety, and this is the name by which he will be called, the Lord our Righteousness" (Jeremiah 23:5-6).

Jehovah-Tsidkenu is a covenant name of God—The Lord our Righteousness. In this Scripture, God says that safety and security result when a righteous king is in authority. He will do what is wise, and just, and right. Righteous authority will address the root issues of man's fallen nature, thus insuring good fruit.

I bless you with knowing that your righteousness was positionally secured in Jesus, but I bless you with putting a high value on pursuing a godly life. I bless you with taking His righteousness and building righteousness into your life, so that you can be a life-giving leader. As you take a position of leadership among your peers and in your community, your level of righteousness will have direct implications for the safety and security of others.

Strong's Greek dictionary says that the word "godliness" is made up of two words that mean "good" or "well" and "to worship." It is all about your heart attitude of worship to God. I bless you, _____, with doing those things that spring from and create a lifestyle of a heart of worship, thereby disciplining yourself for the purpose of godliness. Godliness and righteousness are not behavioral things. I bless you with focusing on the wellspring of your heart out of which you live and make choices. I bless you with a lifestyle that is uncompromisingly based on what Jesus would do, because He is living in you to do your

Father's good and perfect will. I bless you with life-giving wisdom, justice, and righteousness in dealing with everyone. I bless you with doing the right thing because it is the right thing to do based on an inner heart motivation to please your Father.

I bless you with a heart that fights for and shepherds the hearts of others, particularly those in your family. I bless you with looking beyond their outward behavior to their hearts to heal and restore, to affirm and validate. I bless you with eyes to see them as whole and holy in your Savior, and to respond to them as He sees them to be and knows they can be in Him.

I bless you, _____, with righteous authorities who do not compromise your security and safety. I bless you with authorities who will not compromise what is wise, just, and righteous, but will walk according to Micah 6:8 "He has showed you, O man, what is good; And what does the Lord require of you? To act justly and to love mercy and to walk humbly with your God." I bless you with obedience to pray for and bless all in authority so that you and others may live a quiet and peaceful life in all godliness and holiness. This pleases your Father. I bless you with favor with righteous civil government, church leadership, and leadership in the marketplace. I bless you in the name of Jesus, Jehovah-Tsidkenu.

Respond with your spirit...
Write your thoughts, etc.

Day 11 Jehovah-Shammah

_____, listen with your spirit to the Word of God. "...And the name of the city from that time on will be: The Lord is There" (Ezekiel 48:35).

Jehovah-Shammah is a compound covenant name of God. Ezekiel ministered to the exiles in Babylon after Judah had been punished for sinning against God. The prophet foretold the restoration of the political, social, economic, ecological, and spiritual state of all the tribes of Israel. This will result in the reconstruction of the temple, the restoration of priestly service, and the habitation of God once again among his people as His shekinah glory fills the temple. The last phrase of the book of Ezekiel is "the Lord is There." God intended this reality for man from the time of the Garden. Adam and Eve experienced the presence of God as He enjoyed the company of the man and woman he had made. The religious history of mankind is the story of trying to return to God's design, or else manufacturing our own religious days, ceremonies, books, buildings, programs, and songs. God wants us to rediscover the simplicity of the Garden, where His children enjoyed His presence without man-made filters.

_____, I bless you with knowing deeply that you were made for your Father and not the other way around. I bless you with knowing specifically how your Father designed you and what He designed you to do for His kingdom, so that you can contribute to the visible and spiritual world. For you to be famous and successful with your skills is a hollow measure of success. I bless you with the highest pursuit that mankind can attain: experiencing the presence of God. I bless you with pursuing the presence and favor of your Father more than the comforts of life. I bless you with a heart that says that your Father's presence is indispensable to your life's having fulfillment, joy, and

peace. I bless you with faithfully "being there for Him."
I bless you with passing the test of faithfulness in longing for
and pursuing the perspective and presence of God.

I bless you also, _____, with knowing that
your Father is there for you at all times. He is there as
Abba Father, when you need fathering. He is there as the
answer for your uncertainty and questions. He is there for
you as your defender and deliverer when you feel attacked.
He is there as your faithful friend when you feel alone.
He is there as the God of love when you feel unloved and
need a hug. He's there for you as mercy and grace when
you are too hard on yourself or others. He is there for you
with hope when you are discouraged and want to quit. He
is there for you, never-failing, always the same, even when
you are fickle and faithless. He is there as quieter of the
storm for conflicts and fears within your soul. He is there as
true satisfaction when you've tried everything but Him. He
is there as true riches when you are tempted by the world's
allure. He is there as way-maker when there seems to be no
way out. I bless you with proving Him true, over and over
again. I bless you with being certain that He is covenantally
committed to being true to His names and the attributes
by which He has revealed Himself to you. I bless you with
never living a minute without realizing that your Father is
there and that no need or desire of yours can strain His
resources or His willingness to give you His very best. I bless
you in the name of Jehovah-Shammah, your God who is
always there.

Respond with your spirit...
Write your thoughts, etc.

Day 12 Jehovah-M'Kaddesh

_____, listen with your spirit to God's Word for you. "...I am the Lord, who makes you holy" (Leviticus 20:8). "...You will rejoice in the Lord and glory in the Holy One of Israel" (Isaiah 41:16). "Shout aloud and sing for joy, people of Zion, for great is the Holy One of Israel among you" (Isaiah 12:6).

God's holiness is not what He does. "Holy" is who He is, the Holy One. His holiness cannot be separated from who He is. He is without spot or blemish. His eyes are too pure to look on sin. Yet His plan of redemption called for Jesus to take your sins on Himself and die to make you holy in Him. You cannot make yourself holy, no matter how hard you try or how perfectly you live. Your perfection is not holiness. Jesus was the only perfect one who ever walked the earth. The Hebrew word "qadhash" implies being pure, devoted to God, set apart for a special task or the worship of God.

_____, I bless you with knowing your holy Father. I bless you with knowing how His holiness is counted to your credit by the death of Jesus on the cross. I bless you with knowing that nothing you ever do can make Him love you less or love you more. I bless you with freedom from your own perfectionism and the perfectionism of others, because through your Father's eyes, He sees you as perfect in His perfect and beloved Son. I bless you with joy in God's holiness and your own. Our culture does not associate joy with holiness, but God says in His Word that joyful shouting and singing are part of the celebration of who He is. I bless you with celebrating the beauty of His holiness and the glory of your Holy One who accepts you completely and calls forth the best in you.

_____, listen to the Word of God in Isaiah 43:1-3. "But now, this is what the Lord says—he

who created you, O Jacob, he who formed you, O Israel:
'Fear not, for I have redeemed you; I have summoned you
by name; you are mine. When you pass through the waters,
I will be with you; and when you pass through the rivers,
they will not sweep over you. When you walk through the
fire, you will not be burned; the flames will not set you
ablaze. For I am the Lord, your God, the Holy One of Israel,
your Savior…'"

      I bless you with receiving the truth that your Father
treats you with special care because you are set apart
to belong to Him. I bless you with keen consciousness
that you are set apart for Him, for His purposes, for His
pleasure, and to His glory. I bless you with knowing deeply
in your spirit that you are clean, you are dedicated, you are
consecrated to God. I bless you with freedom from anything
that would make you unusable for your Father's glory. I
bless your spirit with being reserved exclusively for heart's
devotion and life's affection to your holy Father. I bless you
with appreciation that your Father knows you by name and
will change the course of rivers and the nature of flames, if
necessary, to keep His holy promises to you to be with you.
I bless you with freedom from fear because of His guarantee
that nothing can destroy you. I bless you with the power
and authority of His names by which He identifies Himself
as your God, your Holy One, and your Savior. I bless you in
the name of Jehovah-M'Kaddesh.

Respond with your spirit…

Write your thoughts, etc.

Day 13 Yahweh

_____, I call your spirit to attention in the covenant-keeping name of Yahweh—the God who is the Self-existent One who has existed before the beginning of time, before anything that we can conceive. He is the God who has sustained everything that He has created. Before the foundation of the world, Yahweh, this self-existent God, willed you into existence. He wrote the story of your life and designed the treasures that you would have. Before He created the world, you were in the mind of Yahweh. Because of His power and because of the nature of who He is, He has chosen to enter into covenant with you. You as a child of Yahweh have the protection and the provision of all of God's resources.

I bless you with knowing the truth of the nature of Yahweh, the truth of the immensity of His love for you. I bless you with experiencing in your spirit, not just knowing in your mind, the all-sufficiency of God. I bless you with seeing in your life His provision as He goes before you, as He makes a way for you, as He brings resources and gifts into your life in many different ways. I bless you with having the eyes of your spirit opened to recognize the gifts that Yahweh gives to you through different means and different people at different times. Yahweh will not always deal with you directly. He will deal with you through others, and I bless you that the eyes of your spirit may recognize the gifts of the covenant-keeping God.

I bless you with celebrating the freedom of the covenant as well as the responsibilities. I bless you with living in a greater level of the covenant than others around you. The covenant blessings are immense, proportionate to the immensity of Yahweh himself. We in our humanity typically only recognize a small portion of our blessings, but I bless you, child of Yahweh, with learning more and more about the covenant conditions and the blessings that are yours and which reflect the immensity of the God who willed you into existence.

I bless you with possessing your birthright. To possess your birthright you will need to receive the blessings of Yahweh. I bless you with experiencing His joy in partnering with you in covenant for you to become everything that He designed you to be. I bless you with experiencing the joy of Yahweh as He celebrates your discovering new facets of yourself, for you are part of God's gift to you. As you discover yourself, you discover how each piece fits together, how each piece brings joy to you. He rejoices over your joy, for the joy of your being you is a reflection of Yahweh's immensity. I bless you, child of Yahweh, with experiencing the full parameters of the covenant to which Yahweh has called you. I bless you in the name of the Father and the Son and the Holy Spirit, Amen.

Respond with your spirit...

Write your thoughts, etc.

Day 14 The Faithful God

_____, I call your spirit to attention in the name of the faithful God. The God who has been faithful to you will continue to be faithful to you. I bless you with God demonstrating his faithfulness in your design. I bless you with God being faithful to complete in your life that which He willed before the foundations of the world. I bless you with Philippians 1:6, which says that "...he who began a good work in you will carry it on to completion...."

> I BLESS YOU WITH PHILIPPIANS 1:6, WHICH SAYS THAT "...HE WHO BEGAN A GOOD WORK IN YOU WILL CARRY IT ON TO COMPLETION...."

Philippians 2:13 says, "For it is God who works in you to will and to act according to his good purpose." I bless you, _____, with experiencing the grace of God to finish the things that God has placed in your heart. There are so many areas where you desire to do the work of God and have not yet finished the work, but I bless you with knowing God's faithfulness in providing the grace to finish as well as the desire.

I bless you with experiencing facets of your redemptive gift that others around you have not experienced and cannot explain. I bless you with being a trailblazer. After the many thousands of years of human history, God has not yet displayed the fullness of the gift that you walk in, and I bless you with experiencing God's faithfulness in bringing facets of your design into fullness in your life in ways that we have not seen in other people with your redemptive gift.

I bless you with experiencing the faithfulness of God in your relationships. Although your relationships in the past have not always been easy or free of pain, I bless you with seeing the fruit of every relationship that God brings into your life, whether painful or overtly life-giving. I bless you with seeing the faithful God at work in relationships.

137

I bless you with experiencing the faithfulness of God in financial provision and material provision. I bless you with not just being comfortable in your life but seeing the provision as coming from the hand of God. I bless you with always being sensitive to the connection between God's gracious giving hand and his faithful giving hand from which you receive on a daily basis.

I bless you with being free from complacency. I bless you with seeing the faithfulness of God in ministry. As you speak to others, may you rejoice on a regular basis with seeing God's divine appointments. May you recognize how God has gone ahead of you to prepare the spirit, the will, and the mind of the people to whom you are ministering. I bless you with seeing the faithfulness of God in giving you insight, understanding, verses, and experiences in your life the day before you need to share them with someone else. I bless you with having your mouth full of fresh manna as the faithful God is there, knowing before you do what you need, and being faithful to provide for you.

I bless you, beloved child of the faithful God, with having the joy of imparting your life message of faithfulness to the next generation and the generation after. I bless you with being able to receive everything that a faithful God wants to give. I bless you with passing on those gifts to others, walking in your responsibility, so that they too can savor the rights that they have in God. I bless you with knowing much of the faithfulness of God as He faithfully fulfills his responsibilities, so that you can know your rights as a blessed child of God, and so that others will be able to draw from your well and taste the faithfulness of God.

I bless you with having the anointing of presence, that causes others in the places you inhabit to have greater faith in the faithfulness of God, and a greater ability to appropriate and incarnate what they have not savored yet.

Your destiny, your birthright, your calling, is to reveal to people a facet of the nature of God that they have not seen yet. This will be catalytic to the rest of the theology that they have. I bless you with knowing the faithfulness of God and with revealing the faithful God to others who have a theological God but need to know a faithful God. I bless you in the name of the Father and the Son and the Holy Spirit, Amen.

Respond with your spirit...

Write your thoughts, etc.

Day 15 The God of Gods

Child of the Most High, I call your spirit to attention in the name of the God of gods. Listen to his Word for you. "For the LORD your God is God of gods and Lord of lords, the great God, mighty and awesome, who shows no partiality and accepts no bribes. He defends the cause of the fatherless and the widow, and loves the alien, giving him food and clothing" (Deuteronomy 10:17-18).

_____, God cares for you from His position of magnificence, from the majesty of being the God of gods and the Lord of lords, because you are a reflection of Him. You are a piece of His greatness. You are a piece of His majesty. You are a reflection of the immensity of Him as He crafted you together in your mother's womb. Although there have been billions of people before you, you are one-of-a-kind. You are unique. You were designed to do things on earth that nobody else can do. There is a deposit of the very nature of God in you that has not been shared with anybody else or replicated in any other person's life. So I bless you, child of the God of gods, to be a reflection, a manifestation, to be a light on earth revealing the facets of the nature of the God that is above all other gods. False gods can destroy, can imitate, but only the true God can create a manifestation of who He is. With your marvelous gifts, with the calling and the anointing on your life, you will walk with powerful men and women and with the most lowly. In the greatness and the smallness, you are visibly incarnating a facet of the enormity and magnificence of the God who shows no partiality.

I bless you and I bless your spirit, child of the God of gods, to understand and to incarnate God who knows no partiality. When the world sees you, they will see justice. They will see someone who is so in tune with God, whom you represent, that no human cultural influence will sway you from your calling and your destiny. I bless you to bring that impartiality wrapped in the package of compassion and attentiveness to the lowly as well as to the great. May it not be an impartiality that is just and harsh, but I bless your spirit and your soul with incarnating the impartiality of God with compassion that befits a child who is a reflection of the God of gods and the Lord of lords.

I bless you as you walk among men and women of power that they would defer to that which is not visible in the natural. I bless you with causing unsaved men and women who do not know the God who made you to defer to the power of God that is manifested in you. I bless your life with experiencing human power deferring to the God of gods who is in you, who is part of you. You are part of Him. You are the incarnation of the ultimate power on earth. I bless you also to be that same incarnation of the power of God wrapped in tenderness to the most fragile, the most vulnerable, the most insecure on Earth.

I bless you with being like the God of gods who presents himself in tenderness without devastating the dimly burning flame that is about to go out. I bless you with being that kind of incarnation of the God of gods to the culture around you, for He made you out of His own substance and essence. I bless you in the name of the Father and of the Son and the Holy Spirit, Amen.

Respond with your spirit...

Write your thoughts, etc.

Day 16 El Shaddai

_____, I call your spirit to attention in the name of El Shaddai, God who is all-sufficient. Listen to His Word for you. "May God Almighty (El Shaddai) bless you and make you fruitful and increase your numbers until you become a community of peoples" (Genesis 28:3). The all-sufficient God has drawn from His nature, from His character, from His sufficiency, and He has made you a very skilled and talented and anointed person. God has drawn from His immensity and equipped you to do many things. But God is calling you into a task that is so much larger than your talents can achieve. God has called you into situations that are humanly impossible, although when compared to others around you, you stand head and shoulders above them. God is doing this as El Shaddai, the God who will provide everything you need, the all-sufficient God who understands the path that He has called you to.

THE SKILL SET THAT GOD HAS GIVEN YOU FROM HIS OWN CHARACTER IS MORE THAN ENOUGH FOR YOU TO BRING LIFE TO MANY INDIVIDUALS, AND YOUR BATTLE IN LIFE WILL BE THE TEMPTATION TO STAY WITH THOSE THINGS THAT YOU DO SO EXCEPTIONALLY WELL, WHERE YOU ARE CELEBRATED, WHERE YOU ARE LOVED, AND WHERE YOU ARE AFFIRMED.

You will be able to do many things through the giftings that God has placed in you from Himself. You will find satisfaction, pleasure, and fruit in using those skills, using them well, being a life-giver, and touching people's lives. Yet continually in the back of your spirit, you will know that God has called you not to deal with individuals, but to deal with community. God has called you in the sum of your life to be an elder and to wrap your arms around a community with huge issues. God has called you to lead the community into wholeness. The skill set that God has given you from His own character is more than enough for you to bring life to many individuals, and your battle in life will be the temptation to stay with those things that you do so exceptionally well, where you are celebrated, where you are loved, and where you are affirmed.

You will not be celebrated for the larger task that God has called you into. You will not be affirmed for it, and you will be told to leave it alone. You will be told that you cannot do it, and that is true. You can only do it as you partner with El Shaddai. God wants you to know two different levels of El Shaddai. Your competence drawn from His character is a beautiful thing, but it is a more beautiful thing when there is a flow of the power, the nature of El Shaddai the all-sufficient God, through you as an elder to your community, bringing wholeness to a group of people, not just individuals. Your Father says to you that you will come up against that situation many times, and He is fully aware that you will fail repeatedly. He knows that you will visit that task that He has placed deep within your spirit, the one you cannot shake off no matter how you try, and that you will fail once and again. Both people and the enemy of God will tell you to leave it alone, because it is too big to be healed.

> I SPEAK THE NAME EL SHADDAI AS A BLESSING OVER YOU, THE CHILD WHO WAS DESIGNED BY GOD AND RAISED UP FOR THIS TASK.

Against that lie, against the bigness of the wound that the enemy left on a people group, I speak the name El Shaddai as a blessing over you, the child who was designed by God and raised up for this task. I bless you with finishing your life with the power of El Shaddai flowing to you and through you. It is His timing. I bless you with experiencing the victory of El Shaddai enabling you to heal that which the world has said cannot be healed. I bless you, beautiful beloved child of El Shaddai, with incarnating in a new way the power of this name of God. Scripture says that you shall not misuse the name of the Lord your God. That tells us that there is a right way to use the name and a right name for the situation. The calling of God on your life is deeply rooted in the name of El Shaddai. Almighty God triumphantly pits the all-sufficiency of His name against the petty wound that the enemy has magnified and amplified. He is all-sufficient for the wound, for the culture, for the community that you have been called to, and for you, blessed child of El Shaddai.

I bless you in the name of the Father and of the Son and of the Holy Spirit, Amen.

Respond with your spirit...

Write your thoughts, etc.

Day 17 Lord Of Hosts

Beloved child of the Most High, I call your spirit to attention in the name of the Lord of hosts, the name that was used by David when he was confronting the spiritual and physical attack of Goliath. God designs, God plans, God intends to work through community, but from time to time the community is so broken, so far from the knowledge of God that they are unable to step up to do what God has called them to do. This was the case in David's day. So from time to time throughout history God raises up individuals who know the Lord of hosts, who know their God, who stand alone in their relationship with God. They speak judgment in the name of the Lord of hosts on behalf of the community against the enemies of God.

David told Goliath that God would give him Goliath's head. God has called you to be in that position at some time during your life. David was a king to the community and had his community of mighty men. There were different communities in different seasons in his life that he was connected to, drew life from, and worked with in a collective way. But there were those moments in his life when he stood alone, connected to the Lord of hosts, and he was to speak judgment and deliverance simultaneously to the people of God.

I bless you with deepening knowledge of the Lord of hosts. I bless you with that handcrafted experience that only God can create. Just as young David learned from God's customized school of hardship how to walk as a man alone, detached from the nation, I bless you with knowing the Lord of hosts to that degree. On those occasions when you have to stand alone, when the community of God has failed to step up as they should, I bless you to be like David. I bless you to be someone who steps back into the community after he has walked in such an unusual position of authority.

You are to be in community, and also to be apart from community, and also to work through community as God decrees and in His times; but when the community has failed to step up, you must be so confident, so certain of your relationship with the Lord of hosts that you can stand as one person, connected with the Lord of hosts, and speak judgment on behalf of the Lord of hosts against His enemies in such a way as to make a public spectacle of the enemy.

We do not have in our theology books a manual for how to groom a person for such a position. We do not have a methodology for teaching someone's spirit to be so attuned to the Spirit of the Lord of hosts that they recognize the voice of the Captain of the Lord of hosts without having to be introduced to Him. But I bless you with being in a school that is unusual, that is unique. I bless you with being in the school of the Lord of hosts as He nurtures you, grooms you, prepares you for that moment or those moments in your life when you stand on behalf of a community that has failed. I bless you to restore order in the heavenlies because you know the Captain of the Lord of hosts. I bless you, beloved child. I bless you, mighty warrior. I bless you, child of the Most High God, with fulfilling your destiny in community and out of community. I bless you in the name of the Father and the Son and the Holy Spirit, Amen.

Respond with your spirit...

Write your thoughts, etc.

Day 18 Abba Father

_____, I call your spirit to attention in the name of Abba Father. Listen to his Word in Galatians 4:6. "Because you are sons, God sent the Spirit of his Son into our hearts, the Spirit who calls out 'Abba, Father'." God desires you to know Him in many different ways in your life, but one of the most foundational is to know Him as Abba Father. He desires that you have an intimate relationship with Him as Father, to understand your rights as a child before you walk in your responsibilities as a steward. The verse clearly says that God sends His Spirit to you, and His Spirit cries out in you before you can cry out for yourself: "Abba Father."

There will be fathers here on earth of greater and lesser skill, but all of them will fall short. Some of them may fall terribly short of the fatherhood of God. Nonetheless, I bless you with a magnificent work by the Spirit of sonship who teaches your spirit how to trust the Father when you have been betrayed by earthly fathers. I bless you with knowing the security and the joy of the Father's relationship with you. I bless you with experiencing deep in your own spirit the joy, the pleasure on the Father's face when you turn to Him, when you leave the commotion of the world and run to Him as a little child would. I bless you with deep healing that comes to your generational lines through experiencing in a multitude of different ways the lessons of the Spirit of sonship. I bless you with seeing the joy of the Father, the wisdom of the Father, the patience of the Father, the kindness of the Father, the creativity of the Father, and the humor of the Father.

Above all else, _____, the name of Abba Father is deeply rooted in security. Where your father may not have kept you safe, where other fathers may even have violated your boundaries, I bless you with full development in your life of that profound sense of safety. This can only come to those who intimately know the heart of their heavenly Father, not just His strength. As God calls you to minister the Father's heart to others throughout the various chapters of your life, I bless you with ministering from a full cup. I bless you with seeing the Father in a myriad of ways and having richly textured teachings about the Father which you present to a needy world.

I bless you with knowing the Father in a way that erases the line between the sacred and the secular. I bless you with seeing Abba Father and having intimacy, safety, joy, and security with Him in the church, out of the church, at work, in your home, in times of pain and times of joy. I bless you with raising the standard in your community for an understanding of Abba Father. I bless the Spirit of sonship that He may do a perfect work in you, releasing the full fragrance of who you are, which can only come from those who have been perfectly fathered. I bless your essence as a person. I bless you with going back to your childhood and filling in the areas that were not properly fathered the first time around. I bless you with celebrating Abba Father by manifesting Him in who you are in your community as a contagious example of someone who has tasted and drunk deeply of the work of the Spirit of sonship. I bless you, beloved child, in the name of the Father and of the Son and the Holy Spirit, Amen.

Respond with your spirit...

Write your thoughts, etc.

Day 19 Ancient of Days

_____, I call your spirit to attention in the name of the Ancient of Days. Listen to his Word in Daniel 7:9-10, 21-27. "As I looked, thrones were set in place, and the Ancient of Days took his seat. His clothing was as white as snow; the hair of his head was white like wool. His throne was flaming with fire, and its wheels were all ablaze. A river of fire was flowing, coming out from before him. Thousands upon thousands attended him; ten thousand times ten thousand stood before him. The court was seated, and the books were opened. As I watched, this horn was waging war against the saints

YOU SERVE THE ANCIENT OF DAYS WHO WILL SIT ON THE THRONE, AND HE WILL DECREE JUSTICE.

and defeating them, until the Ancient of Days came and pronounced judgment in favor of the saints of the Most High, and the time came when they possessed the kingdom. He gave me this explanation: 'The fourth beast is a fourth kingdom that will appear on earth. It will be different from all the other kingdoms and will devour the whole earth, trampling it down and crushing it. The ten horns are ten kings who will come from this kingdom. After them another king will arise, different from the earlier ones; he will subdue three kings. He will speak against the Most High and oppress his saints and try to change the set times and the laws. The saints will be handed over to him for a time, times and half a time. But the court will sit, and his power will be taken away and completely destroyed forever. Then the sovereignty, power and greatness of the kingdoms under the whole heaven will be handed over to the saints, the people of the Most High. His kingdom will be an everlasting kingdom, and all rulers will worship and obey Him.' "

This, child of the Ancient of Days, is your birthright. This is what God has called you to. You serve the Ancient of Days who will sit on the throne, and He will decree justice. His justice is not just to defeat the enemy, but to give the treasures of the enemy to his children, the saints, to rule over.

I bless you to know the greatness and the power of the Ancient of Days, to the limits of the finite mind's capacity, but also, much more deeply in your spirit. I bless you to understand the authority that comes from knowing the uncreated God, God who was before time, God who is greater than any created being. I bless you

I BLESS YOU WITH SEEING YOURSELF AS THE ANCIENT OF DAYS SEES YOU, THE HEIR TO THE AUTHORITY THAT WILL BE DISTRIBUTED AMONG MEN AND WOMEN.

to understand that you are beloved by the Ancient of Days who calls Satan His enemy. I bless you with understanding in your spirit that you are an heir to great authority. I bless you with understanding that God is aching for the day when thrones will be set in place and He sits on that throne to judge His enemies.

_____, don't look at the circumstances of life. There will be seasons when the enemy will prevail and it seems as though God is not intervening, but I beg you to look with your spirit at the Ancient of Days who transcends those short seasons when He allows the enemy to act as though he is in control. You are in the eye of the Ancient of Days. He watches you. He cares for you. He is not grooming you for survival, but for triumph. He is grooming you to be a leader.

I bless you. I bless you with lifting your eyes high against every work of the enemy that has come in and will come into your life. I bless you with seeing yourself as the Ancient of Days sees you, the heir to the authority that will be distributed among men and women. I bless you to stand outside the short perspective of earth time and to see that the Ancient of Days wrote the first chapter, and He has already written the final chapter. In the final chapter you will be free, and you will be in a position of dominion and authority. I bless your spirit to rise above everything that life brings your way and to know in your spirit, in a way that your mind cannot know, the greatness of your heritage. I bless you, beloved beautiful child of the Ancient of Days, with knowing who you are and your heritage and your calling, and with looking beyond the seasons when the enemy has authority. I bless you in the name of the Father and of the Son and of the Holy Spirit, Amen.

Respond with your spirit...

Write your thoughts, etc.

Day 20 God of the Spirits of All Mankind

_____, I call your spirit to attention. Listen to the blessing of the Lord. "The Lord be with your spirit. Grace be with you" (2 Timothy 4:22). I bless you in the name of the God of the spirits of all mankind, as He is called in Numbers 16:22. "But Moses and Aaron fell facedown and cried out, 'O God, God of the spirits of all mankind...'."

Your Father is the God of the spirits of all mankind. The Lord who stretched out the heavens and laid the foundation of the earth is the God who forms the spirit of man. He stirs up your spirit and moves your spirit. Commit your spirit to your Father and Creator (Psalm 35:15), for in His providence He watches over your spirit. I bless you with the knowledge that God gave you life and shows you His unfailing love, and He preserves your life and times by His care (Job 10:12).

> OUR LORD JESUS PRAYED FOR YOU, THAT YOU MAY BE ONE, JUST AS THE FATHER WAS IN HIM AND HE IS IN YOU. BE BLESSED, FOR THE LORD JESUS HAS GIVEN YOU THE GLORY THAT FATHER GOD GAVE HIM, SO THAT YOU MAY BE ONE AS THEY ARE ONE.

_____, listen with your spirit to God's Word. "The first man Adam became a living being; the last Adam, a life-giving spirit" (1 Corinthians 15:45). 1 Corinthians 6:17 states, "But he who unites himself with the Lord is one with Him in spirit." Our Lord Jesus prayed for you, that you may be one, just as the Father was in Him and He is in you. Be blessed, for the Lord Jesus has given you the glory that Father God gave him, so that you may be one as they are one (John 17:20-23). I bless you with uniting yourself with the Lord Jesus, with being one with Him in spirit and being a life-giving spirit to all you meet. I bless you with spiritual fervor, that you may speak and teach accurately the things of the Lord and be diligent and enthusiastic in serving Him, being one with Him and devoted to Him in spirit, soul, and body (Acts 18:25, Romans 12:11, 1 Corinthians 7:34).

"For the word of God is living and active. Sharper than any double-edged sword, it penetrates even to dividing soul and spirit, joint and marrow; it judges the thoughts and attitudes of the heart" (Hebrews 4:12). I bless you with being able to distinguish your spirit from your soul. I bless you to be able to differentiate between the thoughts of your spirit and the attitudes of your soul. I bless you with being able to relate to others spirit to spirit. I bless you with responding to situations and circumstances from the depths of your spirit, not from your soul. I bless you with being humble, contrite, and repentant, so that you will be revived and renewed in heart and spirit by the Holy One, who inhabits eternity (Isaiah 57:15). When you are overwhelmed and your spirit grows faint, I bless you with assurance that He knows the way you should go (Psalm 142:3). When you have troubles, I bless you with the confidence that when you call for help, the Father of your spirit hears you, because He is close to the brokenhearted and rescues those who are crushed in spirit (Psalm 34:18).

> I BLESS YOU WITH GLORIFYING GOD IN YOUR BODY AND YOUR SPIRIT, WHICH ARE GOD'S, BECAUSE YOU ARE BOUGHT WITH A PRICE.

I bless your spirit with being refreshed by others who are faithful to you, and I bless you with often being a refreshment to others in their spirits (1 Corinthians 16:18, 2 Corinthians 7:13). I bless you with the spirit of power, of love and of self-discipline given by God, not of timidity or fear (2 Timothy 1:7).

I bless you with glorifying God in your body and
your spirit, which are God's, because you are bought with
a price (1 Corinthians 6:20 NKJV). I bless you with praying
and singing and praising God with your spirit (1 Corinthians
14:14-16). I bless you with exalting the Lord and rejoicing
in God your Savior with your spirit, as you celebrate His
choosing you and recall all the great things He has done for
you (Luke 1:46-49). I bless you with worshiping the Father
in spirit and truth (John 4:23-24). I bless you in the name of
the God of the spirits of all mankind.

Respond with your spirit...

Write your thoughts, etc.

Day 21 Father of Our Spirits

_____, I call your spirit to attention. Listen to the blessing of the Lord. "The grace of the Lord Jesus Christ be with your spirit" (Philemon 25). I bless you in the name of the Father of our spirits, as He is called in Hebrews 12:9. "We have all had human fathers who disciplined us and we respected them for it. How much more should we submit to the Father of our spirits and live!"

Listen to the Word of God to you. "...The Lord, who stretches out the heavens, who lays the foundation of the earth, and who forms the spirit of man within him..." (Zechariah 12:1). "I will give you a new heart and put a new spirit in you; I will remove from you your heart of stone and give you a heart of flesh" (Ezekiel 36:26). I bless you with the understanding that your Creator, your heavenly Father, created and formed your spirit. I bless you with realizing that the very essence of who you are was placed deep within your spirit before the foundation of the earth were laid. Within your spirit you carry the DNA of your heavenly Father. I bless you with a lifetime and lifestyle of discovering the very character and nature of your Father and Christ in you, the hope of glory. In discovering who God is, you uncover and awaken your spirit to who you are in Him. I bless you with the good gift of God of an undivided heart, right desires, and a new spirit. I bless you with repentance from rebellion and offenses, and I bless you with singleness and tenderness of heart to obey God as one who is truly His (Ezekiel 11:19, 18:31, 36:26).

_____, I bless you with being able to differentiate between your soul and your spirit (Hebrews 4:12). I bless you with distinguishing yourself from those of this world because of the excellent spirit, knowledge, and understanding your Father has placed within you (Daniel 5:12, 6:3). I bless you with knowing that it is the spirit in a man, the breath of the Almighty, that gives you understanding (Job 32:8). I bless you with wholeheartedness and loyalty to your Father in your spirit that is different than it is in others, so that all His good promises of blessings can be yours and you will have a full, rich, spiritual inheritance (Numbers 14:24). I bless you with renewal of your spirit in the Lord (Ephesians 4:23). I bless you with being an example to the others in word, in conduct, in love, in spirit, in faith, and in purity (1 Timothy 4:12 NKJV).

I bless you with the promise from your Lord Jesus that he gives you the words Father God gave Him. I bless you with knowing that you are filled with His words, and your spirit within you compels you to release them with great joy and expectation (Job 32:18).

I bless you with realizing your need for God, for He promises that the kingdom of heaven will be given to you (Matthew 5:3). I bless you with being steadfast and fixed upon God (Psalm 51:10). I bless you with the presence of the Holy Spirit who restores to you the joy of your salvation and makes you willing to live consistently in obedience to Him and harmony with Him (Psalm 51:12). I bless you with commitment to guard your spirit to keep godly covenants with family members (Malachi 2:15-16).

I bless you with a spirit in whom there is no deceit (Psalm 32:2). I bless you with a spirit that is totally committed to the God of truth (Psalm 31:5.) I bless you with the inner unfading beauty of a gentle and quiet spirit, which is of great worth in God's sight (1 Peter 3:4). I bless you with a spirit that yearns for God in the night and longs for Him in the morning (Isaiah 26:9). I bless you with becoming strong in spirit, filled with wisdom and the grace of God (Luke 2:40 NKJV). I bless you in the name of the Father of your spirit.

Respond with your spirit...
Write your thoughts, etc.

APPENDIX
SCRIPTURES ON THE SPIRIT OF MAN

The spirit of man can be:

In anguish
Exodus 6:9 NKJV "So Moses spoke thus to the children of Israel; but they did not heed Moses, because of anguish of spirit and cruel bondage."
Job 7:11 "Therefore I will not keep silent; I will speak out in the anguish of my spirit, I will complain in the bitterness of my soul."

Willing
Exodus 35:21 NKJV "Then everyone came whose heart was stirred, and everyone whose spirit was willing…."
Psalm 51:12 "Restore to me the joy of your salvation and grant me a willing spirit, to sustain me."
Matthew 26:41 "Watch and pray so that you will not fall into temptation. The spirit is willing, but the body is weak."
Mark 14:38 "Watch and pray so that you will not fall into temptation. The spirit is willing, but the body is weak."

Different
Numbers 14:24 "But because my servant Caleb has a different spirit and follows me wholeheartedly, I will bring him into the land he went to, and his descendants will inherit it."

Stubborn
Deuteronomy 2:30 "But Sihon king of Heshbon refused to let us pass through. For the Lord your God had made his spirit stubborn and his heart obstinate in order to give him into your hands, as he has now done."

Sorrowful
1 Samuel 1:15 NKJV "But Hannah answered and said, 'No, my lord, I am a woman of sorrowful spirit. I have drunk neither wine nor intoxicating drink, but have poured out my soul before the Lord.'"

Sullen
1 Kings 21:5 NKJV "But Jezebel his wife came to him, and said to him, 'Why is your spirit so sullen that you eat no food?'"

Passed to someone else
2 Kings 2:9 "When they had crossed, Elijah said to Elisha, 'Tell me, what can I do for you before I am taken from you?' 'Let me inherit a double portion of your spirit,' Elisha replied."
2 Kings 2:15 "The company of the prophets from Jericho, who were watching, said, 'The spirit of Elijah is resting on Elisha.' And they went to meet him and bowed to the ground before him."

Stirred up
1 Chronicles 5:26 "So the God of Israel stirred up the spirit of Pul king of Assyria…"
2 Chronicles 21:16 NKJV "Moreover the Lord stirred up against Jehoram the spirit of the Philistines and the Arabians who were near the Ethiopians."
Ezra 1:1 KJV "Now in the first year of Cyrus king of Persia, that the word of the Lord by the mouth of Jeremiah might be fulfilled, the Lord stirred up the spirit of Cyrus king of Persia, so that he made a proclamation throughout all his kingdom, and also put it in writing…"

Moved
Ezra 1:5 NASB "Then the heads of fathers' households of Judah and Benjamin and the priests and the Levites arose, even everyone whose spirit God had stirred to go up and rebuild the house of the Lord which is in Jerusalem."
John 11:33 "When Jesus saw her weeping, and the Jews who had come along with her also weeping, he was deeply moved in spirit and troubled."

Poisoned
Job 6:4 "The arrows of the Almighty are in me, my spirit drinks in their poison; God's terrors are marshaled against me."

Watched over
Job 10:12 "You gave me life and showed me kindness, and in your providence watched over my spirit."

Turned against God
Job 15:13 NKJV "That you turn your spirit against God, and let such words go out of your mouth?"

Broken
Job 17:1 "My spirit is broken, my days are cut short, the grave awaits me."
Psalm 51:17 "The sacrifices of God are a broken spirit; a broken and contrite heart, O God, you will not despise."
Psalm 76:12 "He breaks the spirit of rulers; he is feared by the kings of the earth."
Isaiah 65:14 "My servants will sing out of the joy of their hearts, but you will cry out from anguish of heart and wail in brokenness of spirit."

Committed to God
Psalm 31:5 "Into your hands I commit my spirit; redeem me, O Lord, the God of truth."

Crushed
Psalm 34:18 "The Lord is close to the brokenhearted and saves those who are crushed in spirit."
Proverbs 15:4 "The tongue that brings healing is a tree of life, but a deceitful tongue crushes the spirit."
Proverbs 15:13 "A happy heart makes the face cheerful, but heartache crushes the spirit."
Proverbs 17:22 "A cheerful heart is good medicine, but a crushed spirit dries up the bones."

Steadfast
Psalm 51:10 "Create in me a pure heart, O God, and renew a steadfast spirit within me."

Faint
Psalm 77:3 "I remembered you, O God, and I groaned; I mused, and my spirit grew faint."
Psalm 142:3 "When my spirit grows faint within me, it is you who know my way."
Psalm 143:4 "So my spirit grows faint within me; my heart within me is dismayed."

Faint cont...
Isaiah 57:16 "I will not accuse forever, nor will I always be angry, for then the spirit of man would grow faint before me—the breath of man that I have created."
Ezekiel 21:7 "And when they ask you, 'Why are you groaning?' you shall say, 'Because of the news that is coming. Every heart will melt and every hand go limp; every spirit will become faint and every knee become as weak as water.' It is coming! It will surely take place, declares the Sovereign Lord."

Inquiring
Psalm 77:6 "I remembered my songs in the night. My heart mused and my spirit inquired..."

Not faithful
Psalm 78:8 "They would not be like their forefathers—a stubborn and rebellious generation, whose hearts were not loyal to God, whose spirits were not faithful to him."

Faithful
Proverbs 11:13 NKJV "A talebearer reveals secrets, but he who is of a faithful spirit conceals a matter."

Weighed by the Lord
Proverbs 16:2 NKJV "All the ways of a man are pure in his own eyes, but the Lord weighs the spirits."

Haughty
Proverbs 16:18 "Pride goes before destruction, a haughty spirit before a fall."

Lowly
Proverbs 16:19 "Better to be lowly in spirit and among the oppressed than to share plunder with the proud."
Proverbs 29:23 "A man's pride brings him low, but a man of lowly spirit gains honor."
Isaiah 57:15 "For this is what the high and lofty One says—he who lives forever, whose name is holy: 'I live in a high and holy place, but also with him who is contrite and lowly in spirit, to revive the spirit of the lowly and to revive the heart of the contrite.'"

160

Ruled
Proverbs 16:32 NKJV "He who is slow to anger is better than the mighty, and he who rules his spirit than he who takes a city."

Calm
Proverbs 17:27 NKJV "He who has knowledge spares his words, and a man of understanding is of a calm spirit."

Searched by the Lord
Proverbs 20:27 "The lamp of the Lord searches the spirit of a man; it searches out his inmost being."

Unruled
Proverbs 25:28 NKJV "Whoever has no rule over his own spirit is like a city broken down, without walls."

Patient
Ecclesiastes 7:8 NKJV "The end of a thing is better than its beginning; The patient in spirit is better than the proud in spirit."

Provoked
Ecclesiastes 7:9 "Do not be quickly provoked in your spirit, for anger resides in the lap of fools."
Acts 17:16 NKJV "Now while Paul waited for them at Athens, his spirit was provoked within him when he saw that the city was given over to idols."

Wayward
Isaiah 29:24 "Those who are wayward in spirit will gain understanding; those who complain will accept instruction."

Distressed
Isaiah 54:6 "'The Lord will call you back as if you were a wife deserted and distressed in spirit—a wife who married young, only to be rejected,' says your God."

Despairing
Isaiah 61:3 "...And provide for those who grieve in Zion—to bestow on them a crown of beauty instead of ashes, the oil of gladness instead of mourning, and a garment of praise instead of a spirit of despair. They will be called oaks of righteousness, a planting of the Lord for the display of his splendor."

Contrite

Isaiah 66:2 "'Has not my hand made all these things, and so they came into being?' declares the Lord. 'This is the one I esteem: he who is humble and contrite in spirit, and trembles at my word.'"

Revived

Isaiah 57:15 "For this is what the high and lofty One says—he who lives forever, whose name is holy: 'I live in a high and holy place, but also with him who is contrite and lowly in spirit, to revive the spirit of the lowly and to revive the heart of the contrite.'"

New

Ezekiel 11:19 "I will give them an undivided heart and put a new spirit in them; I will remove from them their heart of stone and give them a heart of flesh."
Ezekiel 18:31 "Rid yourselves of all the offenses you have committed, and get a new heart and a new spirit. Why will you die, O house of Israel?"
Ezekiel 36:26 "I will give you a new heart and put a new spirit in you; I will remove from you your heart of stone and give you a heart of flesh."

Excellent

Daniel 5:12 NKJV "Inasmuch as an excellent spirit, knowledge, understanding, interpreting dreams, solving riddles, and explaining enigmas were found in this Daniel, whom the king named Belteshazzar, now let Daniel be called, and he will give the interpretation."
Daniel 6:3 NKJV "Then this Daniel distinguished himself above the governors and satraps, because an excellent spirit was in him; and the king gave thought to setting him over the whole realm."

Hardened with pride

Daniel 5:20 NKJV "But when his heart was lifted up, and his spirit was hardened in pride, he was deposed from his kingly throne, and they took his glory from him."

Grieved
Daniel 7:15 NKJV "I, Daniel, was grieved in my spirit within my body, and the visions of my head troubled me."

False
Micah 2:11 NKJV "If a man should walk in a false spirit and speak a lie, saying, 'I will prophesy to you of wine and drink,' even he would be the prattler of this people."

Guarded
Malachi 2:15 "Has not the Lord made them one? In flesh and spirit they are his. And why one? Because he was seeking godly offspring. So guard yourself in your spirit, and do not break faith with the wife of your youth."
Malachi 2:16 "'I hate divorce,' says the Lord God of Israel, 'and I hate a man's covering himself with violence as well as with his garment,' says the Lord Almighty. So guard yourself in your spirit, and do not break faith."

Anxious
Daniel 2:3 NKJV "And the king said to them, 'I have had a dream, and my spirit is anxious to know the dream.'"

Poor
Matthew 5:3 "Blessed are the poor in spirit, for theirs is the kingdom of heaven."

Troubled
John 13:21 "After he had said this, Jesus was troubled in spirit and testified, 'I tell you the truth, one of you is going to betray me.'"
Daniel 2:1 NKJV "Now in the second year of Nebuchadnezzar's reign, Nebuchadnezzar had dreams; and his spirit was so troubled that his sleep left him."

Saved
1 Corinthians 5:5 "Hand this man over to Satan, so that the sinful nature may be destroyed and his spirit saved on the day of the Lord."

One with the Lord
1 Corinthians 6:17 "But he who unites himself with the Lord is one with him in spirit."

Received by God
Acts 7:59 "While they were stoning him, Stephen prayed, 'Lord Jesus, receive my spirit.'"

Formed by God
Zechariah 12:1 "This is the word of the Lord concerning Israel. The Lord, who stretches out the heavens, who lays the foundation of the earth, and who forms the spirit of man within him, declares...."

Fervent
Acts 18:25 NKJV "This man had been instructed in the way of the Lord; and being fervent in spirit, he spoke and taught accurately the things of the Lord, though he knew only the baptism of John."
Romans 12:11 NKJV "Not lagging in diligence, fervent in spirit, serving the Lord"

Stuporous
Romans 11:8 "As it is written: 'God gave them a spirit of stupor, eyes so that they could not see and ears so that they could not hear, to this very day.'"

Devoted to the Lord
1 Corinthians 7:34 "And his interests are divided. An unmarried woman or virgin is concerned about the Lord's affairs: Her aim is to be devoted to the Lord in both body and spirit. But a married woman is concerned about the affairs of this world—how she can please her husband.

Alive
Romans 8:10 "But if Christ is in you, your body is dead because of sin, yet your spirit is alive because of righteousness."

Gentle
1 Corinthians 4:21 "What do you prefer? Shall I come to you with a whip, or in love and with a gentle spirit?"

Present in spirit
1 Corinthians 5:3 "Even though I am not physically present, I am with you in spirit. And I have already passed judgment on the one who did this, just as if I were present."
1 Corinthians 5:4 "When you are assembled in the name of our Lord Jesus and I am with you in spirit, and the power of our Lord Jesus is present."

Given up
Matthew 27:50 "And when Jesus had cried out again in a loud voice, he gave up his spirit."
John 19:30 "When he had received the drink, Jesus said, 'It is finished.' With that, he bowed his head and gave up His spirit."

Committed to God
Luke 23:46 "Jesus called out with a loud voice, 'Father, into your hands I commit my spirit.' When he had said this, he breathed his last."

Subject to control of the prophets
1 Corinthians 14:32 "The spirits of prophets are subject to the control of prophets."

Life-giving
1 Corinthians 15:45 "So it is written: 'The first man Adam became a living being'; the last Adam, a life-giving spirit."

Refreshed
2 Corinthians 7:13 "By all this we are encouraged. In addition to our own encouragement, we were especially delighted to see how happy Titus was, because his spirit has been refreshed by all of you."
1 Corinthians 16:18 "For they refreshed my spirit and yours also. Such men deserve recognition."

Contaminated
2 Corinthians 7:1 "Since we have these promises, dear friends, let us purify ourselves from everything that contaminates body and spirit, perfecting holiness out of reverence for God."

Renewed
Ephesians 4:23 NKJV "And be renewed in the spirit of your mind."

United
Philippians 1:27 "Whatever happens, conduct yourselves in a manner worthy of the gospel of Christ. Then, whether I come and see you or only hear about you in my absence, I will know that you stand firm in one spirit, contending as one man for the faith of the gospel."

Present
Colossians 2:5 "For though I am absent from you in body, I am present with you in spirit and delight to see how orderly you are and how firm your faith in Christ is."

Timid, or powerful, loving and self-disciplined
2 Timothy 1:7 "For God did not give us a spirit of timidity, but a spirit of power, of love and of self-discipline."

Kept blameless
1 Thessalonians 5:23 "May God himself, the God of peace, sanctify you through and through. May your whole spirit, soul and body be kept blameless at the coming of our Lord Jesus Christ."

Made perfect
Hebrews 12:23 "…You have come to God, the judge of all men, to the spirits of righteous men made perfect."

An example
1 Timothy 4:12 NKJV "Let no one despise your youth, but be an example to the believers in word, in conduct, in love, in spirit, in faith, in purity."

Distinguished from soul
Hebrews 4:12 "For the word of God is living and active. Sharper than any double-edged sword, it penetrates even to dividing soul and spirit, joints and marrow; it judges the thoughts and attitudes of the heart."

Gentle and quiet
1 Peter 3:4 "Instead, it should be that of your inner self, the unfading beauty of a gentle and quiet spirit, which is of great worth in God's sight."

The spirit of man can:

Answer
Job 20:3 NKJV "I have heard the rebuke that reproaches me, and the spirit of my understanding causes me to answer."

Give understanding
Job 32:8 "But it is the spirit in a man, the breath of the Almighty, that gives him understanding."

Compel
Job 32:18 "For I am full of words, and the spirit within me compels me."

Have no deceit
Psalm 32:2 "Blessed is the man whose sin the Lord does not count against him and in whose spirit is no deceit."

Sustain him
Proverbs 18:14 "A man's spirit sustains him in sickness, but a crushed spirit who can bear?"

Fail
Psalm 143:7 "Answer me quickly, O Lord; my spirit fails. Do not hide your face from me or I will be like those who go down to the pit."

Rise against you
Ecclesiastes 10:4 NKJV "If the spirit of the ruler rises against you, do not leave your post; for conciliation pacifies great offenses."

Long for God
Isaiah 26:9 "My soul yearns for you in the night; in the morning my spirit longs for you. When your judgments come upon the earth, the people of the world learn righteousness."

Find life
Isaiah 38:16 "Lord, by such things men live; and my spirit finds life in them too. You restored me to health and let me live.

Follow their own spirit
Ezekiel 13:3 "This is what the Sovereign Lord says: Woe to the foolish prophets who follow their own spirit and have seen nothing!"

Know
Mark 2:8 "Immediately Jesus knew in his spirit that this was what they were thinking in their hearts, and he said to them, 'Why are you thinking these things?'"

Sigh deeply
Mark 8:12 NKJV "But he sighed deeply in his spirit, and said, 'Why does this generation seek a sign? Assuredly, I say to you, no sign shall be given to this generation.'"

Rejoice
Luke 1:47 "And my spirit rejoices in God my Savior."

Become strong
Luke 1:80 "And the child grew and became strong in spirit; and he lived in the desert until he appeared publicly to Israel."
Luke 2:40 NKJV "And the child grew and became strong in spirit, filled with wisdom; and the grace of God was upon him."

Return
Luke 8:55 "Her spirit returned, and at once she stood up. Then Jesus told them to give her something to eat."

Worship
John 4:23 "Yet a time is coming and has now come when the true worshipers will worship the Father in spirit and truth, for
John 4:24 "God is spirit, and his worshipers must worship in spirit and in truth."

Serve
Romans 1:9 NKJV "For God is my witness, whom I serve with my spirit in the gospel of his Son, that without ceasing I make mention of you always in my prayers."

Know the thoughts of a man
1 Corinthians 2:11 "For who among men knows the thoughts of a man except the man's spirit within him? In the same way no one knows the thoughts of God except the Spirit of God."

Glorify God
1 Corinthians 6:20 NKJV "For you were bought at a price; therefore glorify God in your body and in your spirit, which are God's."

Utter mysteries
1 Corinthians 14:2 "For anyone who speaks in a tongue does not speak to men but to God. Indeed, no one understands him; he utters mysteries with his spirit."

Pray and sing
1 Corinthians 14:14 "For if I pray in a tongue, my spirit prays, but my mind is unfruitful."
1 Corinthians 14:15 "So what shall I do? I will pray with my spirit, but I will also pray with my mind; I will sing with my spirit, but I will also sing with my mind."

Praise God
1 Corinthians 14:16 "If you are praising God with your spirit, how can one who finds himself among those who do not understand say 'Amen' to your thanksgiving, since he does not know what you are saying?"

Have no rest
2 Corinthians 2:13 NKJV "I had no rest in my spirit, because I did not find Titus my brother; but taking my leave of them, I departed for Macedonia."

Not exploitive
2 Corinthians 12:18 "I urged Titus to go to you and I sent our brother with him. Titus did not exploit you, did he? Did we not act in the same spirit and follow the same course?"

Names of God

God of the spirits of all mankind
Numbers 16:22 "But Moses and Aaron fell facedown and cried out, 'O God, God of the spirits of all mankind, will you be angry with the entire assembly when only one man sins?'"
Numbers 27:16 "May the Lord, the God of the spirits of all mankind, appoint a man over this community."

Father of our spirits
Hebrews 12:9 "Moreover, we have all had human fathers who disciplined us and we respected them for it. How much more should we submit to the Father of our spirits and live!"

Benediction

Galatians 6:18 "The grace of our Lord Jesus Christ be with your spirit, brothers. Amen."

2 Timothy 4:22 "The Lord be with your spirit. Grace be with you."

Philemon 25 "The grace of the Lord Jesus Christ be with your spirit."

CHALLENGE

Ask God to give you blessings for yourself and your family and those to whom you are called to minister. We have had a few "guinea pigs" for receiving these spirit blessings as they have become available. One of our "guinea pigs" wrote this one. She's not Arthur, she's not Sylvia, she's just a true and unique daughter of her Father. She "got it," and you too can write your own spirit blessings.

_____, listen with your spirit to Romans 5:5 "Hope does not disappoint us, because God has poured out His love into our hearts by the Holy Spirit, whom He has given us." The New Living Translation says, "For we know how dearly God loves us, because He has given us the Holy Spirit to fill our hearts with His love."

I bless you with love, unconditional, larger-than-the-universe love, the love of your Father for everybody. May this love permeate in you and through you to your family and everyone around you. I bless you with love that covers a multitude of sins. I bless you with 1 Corinthians 13 love. I bless you with joy. The joy of the Lord is your strength. I bless you with the oil of joy that flows from heaven upon your head dripping down your shoulders until you are totally soaked. I bless you with the manifestation of Christ's joy in you. I bless you with peace, not as the world knows peace, but the peace that is our Lord Jesus Christ. I bless you with putting on the sandals of peace, being prepared at all times to bring the gospel of peace into all circumstances and to all people. I bless you with being a peacemaker, for you are truly the son or daughter of the Most High God. I bless you with long-suffering, not tolerance but patience with yourself and all others. I bless you with knowing that in this long-suffering, God is working in you and in them, bringing about His purposes and plans. May God bless your long-suffering with a holy infusion of your Father's own long-suffering. I bless you with kindness, which is goodness in action. I bless you with a sweet disposition. I bless you with the ability to act for the welfare of those taxing your patience. I bless you with goodness. I bless you with faithfulness that bears all things, believes all things, hopes all things, and endures all things. I bless you with gentleness in dealing with all people, a gentle answer that turns away wrath. I bless you with being wise as a serpent but gentle as a dove. I bless you with self-control. I bless you with a disposition that is even-tempered, tranquil, and balanced in spirit. I bless you with meekness that is power under control. I bless your spirit with the fruit of the Holy Spirit in the name of Jesus Christ our Lord.

Remember that victory doesn't come from having the name of Jesus on our lips but having the very nature of God in our hearts and spirits. Our greatest weapon is the presence of Almighty God. I bless you with not praying for relief but for transformation in all circumstances. I bless your spirit to rise above circumstance to be all God created you to be, not overpowering those around you but calling them as well as yourself to a higher standard.

I bless you with a playful spirit to enjoy your family and others. I bless your spirit with being in control of your flesh and mind, to be free of the restrictions of others and the world. I bless your spirit to fly as an eagle, soaring high, free, and majestic. I bless you in the name of the Spirit of the Lord, in whom there is liberty. Amen.

With the Blessings of Your Father
Blessings Written by:
Arthur Burk: Day 1,2, 3, 4, 6, 7, 8, 9, 11, 12, 13, 14, 15, 16, 17, 18, 19, 20, 21, 22, 23, 24, 25, 26, 27, 28, 29, 30
Sylvia Gunter: Day 5, 10, 31, 32, 33, 34, 35, 36, 37, 38, 40
Sylvia Gunter and Debbie Sample: Day 39

With the Names of God
Blessings Written by:
Arthur Burk: Day 2, 4, 6, 9, 13, 14, 15, 16, 17, 18, 19
Sylvia Gunter: Day 1, 3, 5, 7, 8, 10, 11, 12
Sylvia Gunter and Debbie Sample: Day 20, 21

Cover design and layout by Mae Secrist